Mike Barfield

Illustrated by Lauren Humphrey

THAT'S LIFE!

Looking for the
living things all
around you

Laurence King Publishing

Your Mission: The Case of the Elusive Lifeforms

Key

🔍 Signs of life
(look for this around you)

⚗️ Experiment!

🌐 Number of species
around the world

☆ Superpower

Greetings! I am Sherlock Ohms, the super scientific detective. Join me on a brilliant biological quest: LOOKING FOR THE LIVING THINGS ALL AROUND YOU. Search for the signs of life around you and help reveal the amazing range of organisms present on our planet – including you!

Earth is rife with life. It's everywhere – from the deepest sea beds to the tops of the tallest mountains and beyond. Deserts, rivers, fields and forests all teem with living things, but you can also find life thriving in your home and the world around you.

From microbes to meerkats, turnips to teachers – the variety of living things is mind-boggling. Many are too small to be seen with the naked eye, some you might only see on safari or on TV, but lots are hiding happily all around us.

This book is your guide to the whole wide world of life. Alongside my rodent friends, Ratley and Hattie, I will reveal the identities of Earth's many incredible inhabitants, so you can spot a species and claim: 'That's life!'

Utterly elementary: the meaning of 'life'

Defining 'life' is a big issue for biologists (scientists who study living things). Most agree that living things show the 'seven signs of life', see opposite.

A croc is, therefore, a 'living thing', while a rock is 'non-living'. Biologists also study anything that previously showed the seven signs, such as dinosaurs and other extinct organisms, known only from fossils or dead specimens.

It's good to be alive!

croc

rock

living

non-living

The curious case of coal and chalk

Some non-living materials have a living origin, such as coal (which comes from prehistoric trees) and chalk (from prehistoric plankton). Both are considered non-living, as is the paper this page is printed on – it is made mostly from trees, but it is not alive.

🧪 An open and shut case

All living things move in some way. Watch a daisy growing on a lawn. At dawn, the plant has its petals closed. Slowly, it opens them up to track the sun, closing again at the end of the day. This movement gives the flower its English name: the 'day's eye' – shortened to 'daisy'.

Nutrition

Every organism must acquire food and nutrients to survive. Plants and algae make food through photosynthesis (see page 21), while animals and fungi feed on other living things and their waste, including poo!

Growth

Living things grow, increasing in mass. If you need proof, check out your baby pictures or keep a record of your height over the next few years.

Reproduction

Organisms reproduce to make more organisms to replace those that die, including themselves. Some living things can do this on their own, while others need a mate to create offspring.

The seven signs of life

Movement

All living things move, though you may need a microscope to spot it. For example, bacteria and fungi have tiny moving parts inside their cells invisible to the naked eye. Even plants move – for example, when they grow, bloom and seek out sunlight (see top right).

Sensitivity

The ability of living things to react to changes in their environment, such as in temperature or light.

Respiration

Not to be confused with breathing, this is the way organisms break down chemicals inside their cells to release the energy needed for life. Respiration is what keeps mammals warm.

Excretion

All living things get rid of waste products by excretion. Humans do this through faeces (poo) and urine (wee), as well as through the lungs (in the form of carbon dioxide) and the skin (in the form of sweat).

Life Begins: The Biggest Mystery

The latest clever detective work indicates that life has been on the scene for a very long time. Scientists reckon the Earth was formed from star dust and debris about 4.5 billion years ago. Microscopic fossils suggest life arose soon afterwards, though there is great debate about exactly when and how. Life's precise origins remain a mystery, but the timeline is becoming clearer and may well have been something like this...

There was also intense radiation from space and the young Sun.

4.5 billion years ago

From a mass of molten rocks, the early Earth is cooling and forming a crust. Volcanoes erupt endlessly. Meteorites and asteroids hurtle down from space. Lightning flashes in skies full of space dust, nitrogen, steam and carbon dioxide. Earth is like a giant industrial laboratory, with perfect conditions for producing the chemicals we now associate with life, including organic (carbon-based) compounds and amino acids (the building blocks of proteins).

4.4 billion years ago

The first oceans churn over the angry planet: a vast chemical-rich soup that boils away whenever an asteroid or meteorite strikes it, before eventually raining back to Earth. Below the surface, volcanically hot water streams up through cracks called hydrothermal vents, the heat driving chemical interactions with newly formed rocks and minerals. Above the water, volcanic activity warms shallow pools of chemical soup that lie in impact craters on patches of exposed crust.

Comets may also have brought water and other chemicals.

4.2–3.5 billion years ago

At some unknown moment, in some unknown place, chemistry kickstarts biology. At a hot vent, or maybe in a warm pool, a new chemical substance is made that can form copies of itself. This is the first genetic material – a forerunner of the DNA we know about in chromosomes today (see page 48). Somehow – sooner, later, or possibly at the same time – it is enclosed inside a wall of fat-based molecules (a 'membrane') to form a little bag that can communicate chemically with its environment outside. This new thing gets energy by breaking down chemicals into simpler molecules, and can also replicate itself. It is the first 'cell' – the basic component of all living things.

A self-copying substance inside a tiny bag, along with other chemicals, could have given us the first cell.

STRELLEY POOL, WESTERN AUSTRALIA

This is just one way in which life may have come about. That first cell could have been similar to modern bacteria, including those found living at extreme temperatures around geothermal vents today. There is fossil evidence for bacteria in Australian rocks said to be more than 3.4 billion years old, but many experts think life on Earth began much earlier. Some have also suggested that life came from space, carried by a comet or an asteroid. Earth remains the only place in the universe where we know life exists.

Scientists are running experiments to try and replicate the extreme conditions on early Earth to see if they can produce cells. If they are successful, it would show that life may well have also arisen elsewhere in the universe.

Cells: Little Things Mean a Lot

Cells are the building blocks of life. Every living thing has one or more cells. Since they first emerged, cells have evolved and diversified to give us the many millions of different organisms on our planet today, as well as the billions of different organisms that have lived, died and become extinct since life kicked off.

Together, cells form tissues, tissues combine to form organs, and, ultimately, we get organisms. Cells are stars!

Small and less small

While most cells are microscopic, they can still vary massively in size. The smallest known living thing is a single-celled prokaryotic bacterium called *Mycoplasma genitalium*, just 0.0002 millimetre long. The largest known prokaryote is another bacterium, *Thiomargarita namibiensis*, which can reach roughly the size of the dot at the end of this sentence. Comparing the sizes of the two bacteria is like comparing a bee to a blue whale!

A blue whale has about 100 quadrillion cells, which is 100,000,000,000,000,000!

Two of a kind

Biologists divide cells into two main types depending on whether or not they have a nucleus – a membrane-bound sac containing genetic material.

Simpler cells *without a nucleus* are called 'prokaryotic' and are found in just two kingdoms of life, Archaea (see page 12) and Bacteria (see page 14), both of which are made up of single-celled 'unicellular' lifeforms. The cells of all other living things *have a nucleus* and are called 'eukaryotic'.

There can also be many other differences on top: for instance, cells in plants can photosynthesise (see opposite page), whereas cells of fungi and animals cannot; and eukaryotic organisms can either be single-celled ('unicellular') or have many cells ('multicellular').

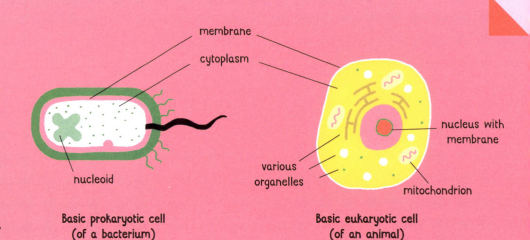

Basic prokaryotic cell
(of a bacterium)

Basic eukaryotic cell
(of an animal)

Cell membrane: contains the cell and controls what passes in and out	**Nucleus:** membrane-bound and containing the genetic material
Cytoplasm: a watery gel containing chemicals, proteins and the various structures ('organelles') that enable cell function	**Organelles:** various structures with different functions within cells
Nucleoid: genetic material without a membrane around it	**Mitochondrion:** provides the cell with energy

Sun trap

Some plant (see page 20) and algae cells (see page 22) contain special organelles called chloroplasts. Inside them, a chemical called chlorophyll uses the energy from sunlight to turn carbon dioxide from the air into sugars that the plant can use as food and for building rigid cell walls.

Known as photosynthesis, this process also releases oxygen for us to breathe. Chlorophyll makes leaves look green, so when you eat lettuce you are literally eating a leafy living power station!

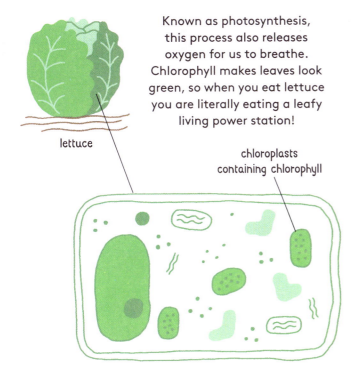

lettuce

chloroplasts containing chlorophyll

What a nerve!

The average human body has about 37 trillion cells – that's 37 followed by 12 zeroes. There are roughly 200 different types of cell, including skin, bone, muscle and fat cells, with red blood cells making up 80% of the total.

The longest single cell in your body is one of the nerve cells ('neurons') making up the sciatic nerve, which runs from the base of your spine down to your big toe. You can measure it with a piece of string. Amazingly, nerve impulses travel along this neuron at over 360 kilometres per hour!

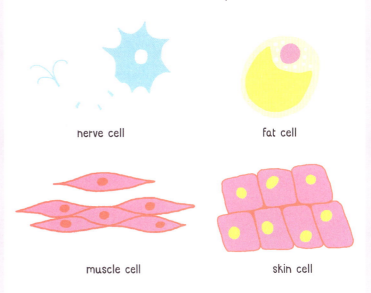

nerve cell

fat cell

muscle cell

skin cell

The single largest eukaryotic cell seen today is the yolk of an unfertilised ostrich egg. A tiny white dot contains the DNA and organelles of the cell, while the huge yolk feeds and protects the developing chick, all contained within a single membrane.

From the first cells, life evolved and developed in complexity. Some 2 billion years ago, early bacteria changed Earth's atmosphere to one rich in oxygen, with new lifeforms evolving that relied on it.

Eukaryotes appear in the fossil record shortly afterwards, along with the first multicellular organisms. The actual timings of these events, however, are the subject of ongoing detective work.

Perhaps one day you will solve the mystery!

The Tree of Life: It's All Relative

From simple beginnings, life has become a lot more complicated and diverse over the past 4 billion or so years. Scientists estimate that there are more than 8 million different species of living things alive today – all of which are descended from the same bacteria-like microbes known as the Last Universal Common Ancestor (LUCA).

Many millions more species have been and gone leaving no record whatsoever, while others exist only as fossils.

In order to study and understand this vast number of organisms, scientists sort them into groups with characteristics in common. This process of identifying, naming and classifying living things is called taxonomy (see page 10).

Several different sorting systems exist, but for the purposes of our detective work we have divided life into the seven kingdoms shown on the opposite page. Three of these contain only simple, single-celled lifeforms (Archaea, Bacteria, Protozoa), the rest are much more complex and multicelled.

The same information used to sort life into these groups can also be used to build a timeline of how life evolved. This is often shown as a 'Tree of Life' – though there are many other ways of representing it.

Lower branches are further back in time, the tips of twigs are species alive today, and the forks of branches represent a shared ancestor. The simplified tree is also a guide to locating the seven kingdoms in this book.

Tree-mendous!

Probably the most significant Tree of Life ever drawn was the rough idea sketched by Charles Darwin in a notebook in 1837. Darwin was developing his theory that new species evolved from earlier ancestors, and wrote next to it: 'I think.'

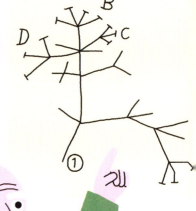

Last Universal Common Ancestor

LUCA was not the first form of life on the planet. It is, however, the one from which all life today developed, beginning with archaea and bacteria. LUCA may well have lived near a hot underwater vent, though other theories exist.

Going viral

A virus is a tiny infectious particle – much smaller than a bacterium – that can invade living cells and get them to make copies of itself. Viruses cause diseases in plants and animals, but, because they can't replicate on their own, they are not generally considered living things. The common cold and influenza ('flu') are caused by viruses, as is Covid-19.

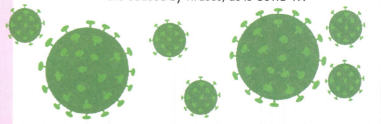

KINGDOM 7: ANIMALIA
PAGE 34

KINGDOM 5: PLANTA
PAGE 20

KINGDOM 6: FUNGI
PAGE 32

KINGDOM 3: PROTOZOA
PAGE 17

KINGDOM 4: CHROMISTA
PAGE 17

PROKARYOTES

KINGDOM 1: ARCHAEA
PAGE 12

KINGDOM 2: BACTERIA
PAGE 14

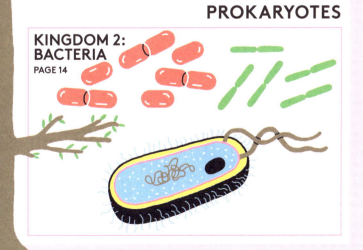

LUCA

The Classification of Life: Sorted

Humans have long tried to organise nature by grouping together similar living things. At first, this was based on appearance and how and where they lived. Today it also includes comparison of their genes.

Using this information, life in this book has been sorted into the seven super-sized gangs (kingdoms) that you have just met on the previous page.

These kingdoms are themselves divided repeatedly into ever smaller groups, each with a special title such as Phylum, Class, Order, Family, Genus and Species. The names tell scientists how similar the members of each group are. Members of a bigger group, such as a phylum, will be alike in some important ways but will differ in others. Members of a class, order and family will be gradually more similar. Members of the same species will be identical. Here are Hattie, Ratley and Ohms to demonstrate:

> Scientific names of organisms are usually given as two words: the genus name (with a capital letter) and then the species name. Both are written in italics and in a form of Latin, for reasons you can find on pages 30–31.

	Mus musculus	*Rattus rattus*	*Homo sapiens*
KINGDOM Mice, rats and humans are all animals.	Animalia	Animalia	Animalia
PHYLUM As growing embryos, mice, rats and humans all develop a small flexible rod called a notochord (see page 47).	Chordata	Chordata	Chordata
CLASS Mammals are furry, warm-blooded and produce milk to suckle their young. Mice, rats and humans are all mammals.	Mammalia	Mammalia	Mammalia
ORDER Hattie and Ratley are rodents, with continuously growing incisor teeth. Humans are primates – along with monkeys, lemurs and apes.	Rodentia	Rodentia	Primates
FAMILY Hattie and Ratley are murids – mouse-like animals. Humans are hominids or 'great apes'.	Muridae	Muridae	Hominidae
GENUS Hattie is a mouse. Ratley is a rat. Humans are, well, human…	*Mus*	*Rattus*	*Homo*
SPECIES 'Musculus' means 'small mouse', 'Rattus' is repeated because that's what the person who invented the name chose for it! And, perhaps surprisingly, given how silly some humans can be, *Homo sapiens* means 'wise man'.	*musculus*	*rattus*	*sapiens*

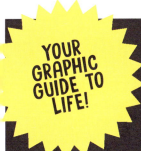

YOUR GRAPHIC GUIDE TO LIFE!

LIFE STORIES

THE FIRST THEORIES: THE CURIOUS CASE OF CREATION

WE HUMANS HAVE LONG PONDERED OUR ORIGINS...

Where did we come from?

That cave over there...

GOOD ANSWER!

BEFORE MODERN SCIENCE, PEOPLE INVENTED STORIES ('CREATION MYTHS') TO EXPLAIN HOW LIFE CAME ABOUT. THE ANCIENT EGYPTIANS, FOR EXAMPLE...

Life emerged from a giant pyramid of mud.

What a filthy idea.

SOUNDS CRAZY? WELL...

NOT SO CRAZY WHEN YOU KNOW THAT MUD FROM THE ANNUAL FLOODING OF THE RIVER NILE KEPT THEIR LANDS FERTILE...

Where have these flowers come from?

It's a blooming miracle!

NATURE WAS A MYSTERY TO PEOPLE, SO THEY LOOKED FOR WAYS TO EXPLAIN IT.

THE ANCIENT GREEKS SAID EARTH WAS A GODDESS CALLED GAIA, BORN FROM A VOID THAT WAS A 'YAWNING NOTHINGNESS'.

'Yawning nothingness'?

Well, I have heard this story lots of times before.

YAWN

STORY OF GAIA

GAIA WAS ALSO KNOWN AS 'MOTHER EARTH'.

SOME FAITHS SHARE THE SAME STORY OF THE WORLD BEING CREATED IN JUST SIX DAYS, WITH THE SEVENTH BEING A DAY OF REST.

DAY 1	DAY 2	DAY 3	DAY 4	DAY 5	DAY 6	DAY 7
DAY, NIGHT.	HEAVEN, EARTH.	LAND, SEA, PLANTS.	SUN, MOON.	BIRDS, FISH.	LAND ANIMALS, HUMANS.	~~DENTIST.~~ REST.

MANY GREAT SCIENTISTS IN THE PAST HAVE BELIEVED THIS, ESPECIALLY IN THE DAYS BEFORE CHARLES DARWIN (SEE PAGES 44–45).

INDEED, IN 1650, A MAN CALLED JAMES USSHER USED THE BIBLE STORY OF GENESIS TO CALCULATE THE PRECISE TIME CREATION HAD BEGUN...

It was about 6pm on 22 October 4004 BCE. Which was, of course, a Saturday!

THE BIBLE

ACCORDING TO USSHER'S CALCULATIONS, THE EARTH TODAY WOULD BE JUST OVER 6,000 YEARS OLD. SOME PEOPLE STILL INSIST THIS IS TRUE.

HOWEVER, FROM STUDYING ROCKS AND FOSSILS, PEOPLE BEGAN TO REALISE THAT THE EARTH WAS VERY MUCH OLDER AND HAD BEEN HOME TO SOME VERY DIFFERENT LIFEFORMS...

Got any plans for tomorrow?

Hmm. Not yet...

A MERE 66 MILLION YEARS AGO (POSSIBLY A SATURDAY...).

IN FACT, BY RADIO-DATING CRYSTALS FOUND IN ROCKS IN AUSTRALIA, GEOLOGISTS HAVE SHOWN THAT THE EARTH IS AT LEAST 4.4 BILLION YEARS OLD...

Er, well, maybe I missed off a few zeroes...

THIS PERIOD OF TIME IS MIND-BLOWINGLY HARD TO IMAGINE, AND HAS BEEN GIVEN A SPECIAL NAME...

We call this 'Deep Time'.

I call this dinner time.

AGE OF EARTH: 4.4 BILLION YEARS

SCIENTISTS GENERALLY ACCEPT THAT THE AMAZING DIVERSITY AND COMPLEXITY OF LIVING THINGS HAVE COME ABOUT BY EVOLUTION OVER BILLIONS OF YEARS, BEGINNING WITH THAT VERY FIRST CELL...

Bit lonely in here by myself...

SOME 3.4 BILLION YEARS AGO OR MORE...

HOWEVER, PEOPLE ARE FREE TO THINK DIFFERENTLY... SOME EVEN BELIEVE THAT LIFE WAS BROUGHT HERE BY ALIENS.

*NOW TO BEGIN OUR WORK...
**BUT IT'S A SATURDAY!

ARGUMENTS ABOUT THE ORIGINS OF LIFE WILL PROBABLY CONTINUE FOREVER – EVEN IF, ONE DAY, SCIENTISTS DO SUCCEED IN CREATING LIFE FROM SCRATCH IN THE LABORATORY...

Still not made any cells yet...

Ah well – that's life! Er...

KINGDOM 1: Archaea

🌐 Over 200 known species

☆ Thrive in extreme environments

Archaea ('AHH-KEE-AH') are single-celled microscopic organisms that look a lot like bacteria (see page 14), but they are different in so many other ways that they have their very own kingdom.

Even though only a few hundred species have been identified, it is thought that Archaea are everywhere on – and inside – Earth, as well as on and inside many organisms, including you! However, unlike bacteria, they are not associated with diseases.

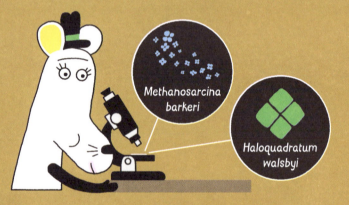

Methanosarcina barkeri

Haloquadratum walsbyi

Smallest of all
Archaea come in some strange shapes and sizes. The smallest known living thing on our planet is an Archaean 'nano-organism' discovered in 2002. Side by side, 2,500 of them would measure about a millimetre!

Hot stuff
Many Archaea are 'extremophiles', thriving in the hottest and harshest environments on Earth, such as around undersea volcanic vents. One Archaea member – *Methanopyrus* – can survive 122°C (the highest recorded temperature for a living thing). This heat-defeating superpower means Archaea are prime candidates for the life we might find on planets such as Mars.

Polluting the planet
Archaea live, alongside other micro-organisms, in the guts of cows, termites and humans. They take waste hydrogen produced by bacteria and use it to make methane gas, an ingredient in farts. While farts are fun, a single cow produces about 250 litres of methane a day – and methane gas in the atmosphere contributes to global warming. That is why some say we should farm fewer cattle and eat less meat and dairy.

Powering the planet
Archaea are used to turn food waste into methane inside giant industrial digesting machines. Rather than being allowed to escape into the air, the methane is burned as a fuel ('biogas'), which is good for the planet as it saves sending food waste to landfill.

🔍 SIGNS OF LIFE:

☐ SKIN

☐ LUNGS

☐ NOSE

☐ GUT (FARTS!)

☐ THERMAL VENTS

☐ SALT LAKES

☐ OCEAN BEDS

☐ ACID MINES

☐ OUTER SPACE?

THE ANCIENT GREEK THINKER ARISTOTLE* IS CONSIDERED THE 'FATHER OF BIOLOGY'...

You can call me 'Dad'...

Coo!

*GREECE, 384–322 BCE.

CURIOUS ABOUT EVERYTHING, ARISTOTLE SPENT MANY YEARS OBSERVING NATURE ON THE ISLAND OF LESBOS...

Ever get the feeling you're being watched?

I can see you!

A GREAT NATURALIST, ARISTOTLE WAS THE FIRST TO CLAIM THAT OCTOPUSES CHANGED COLOUR...

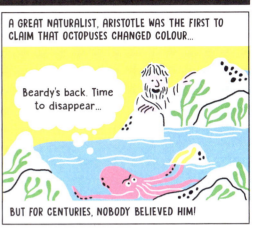

Beardy's back. Time to disappear...

BUT FOR CENTURIES, NOBODY BELIEVED HIM!

AS WELL AS STUDYING ANIMALS IN THE WILD, ARISTOTLE EXAMINED THEIR INSIDES, TOO...

I'm sorry about this...

So are we. Eek!

THE WORLD'S FIRST ZOOLOGIST, HE PUBLISHED HIS WORK IN A FAMOUS TEXT CALLED THE HISTORY OF ANIMALS...

THE HISTORY OF ANIMALS

We're history too, now... SOB!

IT REMAINED THE BIOLOGY BOOK FOR MORE THAN 2,000 YEARS!

IN HIS BOOK, ARISTOTLE DIVIDED ANIMALS INTO THOSE WITH BLOOD* AND THOSE WITHOUT**...

Help! I don't want to be divided!

And I don't want to be without blood!

*VERTEBRATES (WITH BACKBONES).
**INVERTEBRATES (NO BACKBONES).

ANIMALS WERE THEN GROUPED BY THEIR FEATURES. FOR EXAMPLE, ALL BIRDS HAD A BEAK, FEATHERS, WINGS AND TWO LEGS...

Tweet, tweet!

You're fooling nobody, cat...

GROUP MEMBERS THEN VARIED BY SIZE, SHAPE, COLOUR, AND SO ON.

ARISTOTLE ALSO RANKED ALL LIVING AND NON-LIVING THINGS ON EARTH IN ORDER OF SUPERIORITY*...

Lower

higher

*HE CALLED THIS THE GREAT CHAIN OF BEING.

HOWEVER, ONLY HUMANS WERE ACTUALLY CONSIDERED 'PERFECT'.

Of course, I'm perfect!

Perfectly wrong.

AMAZINGLY, PEOPLE ACCEPTED ARISTOTLE'S GREAT CHAIN THEORY FOR MORE THAN 2,000 YEARS, BUT THE IDEA IS NOW DISCREDITED...

Ah, well. Nobody's perfect...

Told you so...

HE WAS, HOWEVER, A BRILLIANT BIOLOGIST – AND HIS CLAIM ABOUT OCTOPUSES IS TRUE!

Ha!

THEY CHANGE COLOUR TO HIDE OR TO STARTLE PREDATORS.

KINGDOM 2: Bacteria

🌐 Possibly 1 million or more species

☆ Abundance

Bacteria are everywhere! In the 2.5 billion years since they appeared, these microscopic single-celled organisms have evolved to exploit every environment on Earth, from icy mountain tops to deep ocean rifts. They've even been found in clouds and on the outside of the International Space Station (ISS). Despite being tiny, these marvellous microbes make up 15% of the total weight of all living things. Only plants on the planet weigh more.

An average human, alone, is home to 39 trillion bacterial cells, which outnumber human cells by about 9 trillion cells. Most of these bacteria live in your digestive system.

Mega-microbe
Being tiny, it took the invention of the microscope to show that bacteria existed (see page 16). The difference in size between an average bacterium and you is similar to the difference between your height and the height at which the ISS orbits Earth (more than 300 kilometres high!).

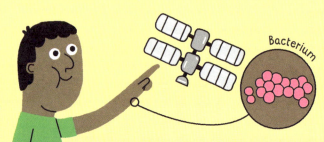

Bacterium

Identity parade
Bacteria come in three main shapes: spheres (cocci), rods (bacilli) and spirals. The shapes are often suggested within their scientific names, and many bacteria form distinctive clusters or chains.

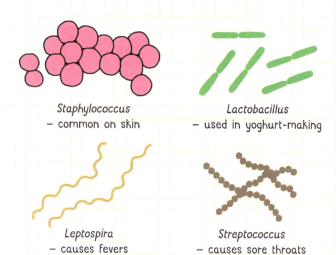

Staphylococcus – common on skin

Lactobacillus – used in yoghurt-making

Leptospira – causes fevers

Streptococcus – causes sore throats

Some bacteria have whip-like 'tails', called 'flagella', to propel themselves. They may also have hair-like projections called 'pili' and an outer coating (capsule), both of which can make them more aggressive in causing disease, and also harder to destroy.

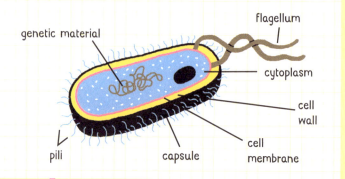

genetic material

flagellum

cytoplasm

cell wall

cell membrane

pili

capsule

On the double
Most bacteria reproduce by growing, copying their genetic material and then splitting in two. *Escherichia coli* (often called, simply, 'E. coli'), a bacterium found in our stomachs, can double its numbers every 20 minutes in ideal conditions.

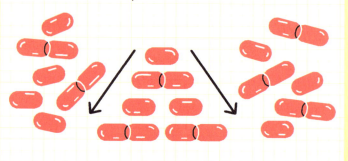

On the menu

Bacteria have an amazing range of foods: living things, dead things, rocks, minerals, oils, plastics, and us! When they grow on or inside other organisms they can cause diseases, some of them seriously harmful. However, special bacteria called cyanobacteria get their energy from photosynthesis, producing oxygen in the process. Billions of years ago, they are thought to have radically changed Earth's atmosphere to one richer in oxygen, more like the air we breathe today. Rocky mounds ('stromatolites') formed by cyanobacteria on the Australian coast are the oldest evidence of life on Earth, dating back at least 3.4 billion years.

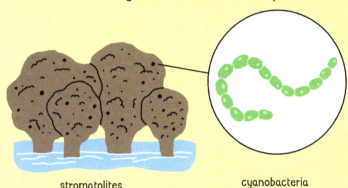

stromatolites   cyanobacteria

Poo and you

Some (unlucky) microbiologists have measured 100 billion bacteria – half of which were still alive – in a single gram of human poo. While these bacteria are fine inside us – and down the loo – spreading them around is a bad idea. Always wash your hands!

Say 'cheese!'

Many fermented foods are made using harmless bacteria, including yoghurt, sauerkraut, kimchi, kefir and soy sauce. Bacteria produce the blue veins in Stilton and Roquefort cheeses and the tastes and textures of many classic cheeses, including Camembert, Gruyère and Brie. *Spirulina*, a cyanobacterium, is sold dried as a health supplement.

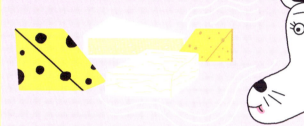

🧪 Grow your own yoghurt

Bring a pan of whole milk almost to the boil (get a grown-up to help), then let it cool to body temperature. Stir in a big spoonful of live yoghurt (check the label), then pour it all into a clean vacuum flask and seal it. Leave it for a day or so and the bacteria will grow and thicken the milk to make yoghurt. Keep it in the fridge after opening.

1 warmed milk   2 live yoghurt   3 vacuum flask

Food for thought

Bacteria are a vital part of the food chain. Some bacteria form special bumps, called 'nodules', in the roots of plants, such as beans and peas. The bacteria take nitrogen from the air and use it to form amino acids, the building blocks of proteins. Other bacteria in the stomachs of cattle and sheep produce vitamin B12, essential for health. People can get this B12 from meat and dairy products, but vegetarians and vegans sometimes need to take a special supplement.

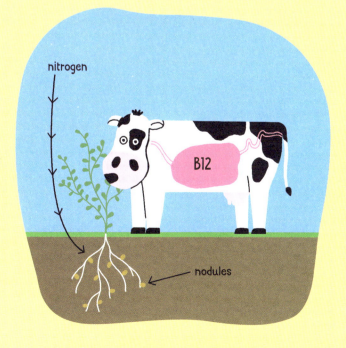

nitrogen

B12

nodules

🔍 SIGNS OF LIFE

- ☐ YOGHURT
- ☐ CHEESES
- ☐ SAUERKRAUT
- ☐ KIMCHI
- ☐ SPIRULINA
- ☐ ME
- ☐ YOU
- ☐ POO
- ☐ EVERYWHERE!

WHEN IT CAME TO ORGANISING ORGANISMS, SIZE PLAYED A BIG PART...

Elephant!

I hate hide and seek...

LARGE ORGANISMS WERE EASY TO OBSERVE. REALLY TINY ONES WENT UNNOTICED.

UNAIDED, THE HUMAN EYE CAN'T SEE THINGS SMALLER THAN ABOUT 0.1 MILLIMETRE...

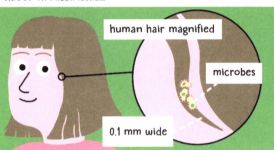

human hair magnified

microbes

0.1 mm wide

...WHICH IS WHY MICROBES (MICROSCOPIC LIFEFORMS) REMAINED UNKNOWN FOR THOUSANDS OF YEARS.

SOME PEOPLE DID SUSPECT THAT 'INVISIBLE MICRO-ORGANISMS' CAUSED DISEASES...

This is called 'germ theory'.

It'll never catch on. AH-CHOO!

IBN SINA (ALSO KNOWN AS AVICENNA), IRAN, c.1035 CE.

HOWEVER, MANY BELIEVED DISEASES WERE JUST CAUSED BY FOUL-SMELLING 'BAD AIR'...

That idea stinks.

It wasn't me...

KNOWN AS 'MIASMA THEORY', IT WAS BALONEY!

THE INVENTION OF THE MICROSCOPE IN THE SEVENTEENTH CENTURY FINALLY REVEALED NATURE IN MINIATURE...

I saw and named the first 'cells'!

FIG. 1

CORK CELL 1665

ROBERT HOOKE, ENGLISH SCIENTIST, 1635-1703.

IN 1676, DUTCH HABERDASHER ANTONIE VAN LEEUWENHOEK* SAW THE FIRST BACTERIA – FROM INSIDE HIS MOUTH!

I call them 'animalcules'.

Microscope

That's a bit of a mouthful.

*DELFT, NETHERLANDS, 1632-1723.

USING HIS SMALL HANDMADE MICROSCOPES, HE DREW LOTS OF PREVIOUSLY UNSEEN MICRO-ORGANISMS...

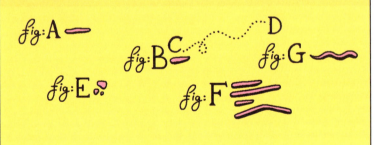

fig:A
fig:B
C
D
fig:E
fig:F
fig:G

BUT PEOPLE STILL DIDN'T BELIEVE SUCH THINGS CAUSED DISEASES.

INSTEAD, THEY FELL FOR MANY OTHER CRAZY NOTIONS, INCLUDING SOME ABOUT THE ORIGINS OF ORGANISMS...

Maggots come from meat.

Mice come from cheese wrapped in rags.

You're crazy! Mice come from wheat!

THIS IDEA WAS KNOWN AS MADNESS 'SPONTANEOUS GENERATION' – LIFE FROM NON-LIVING THINGS.

IT WAS PARTLY ARISTOTLE'S FAULT (SEE PAGE 13)...

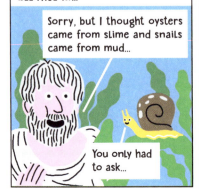

Sorry, but I thought oysters came from slime and snails came from mud...

You only had to ask...

IN 1668, ITALIAN PHYSICIAN FRANCESCO REDI* PROVED MAGGOTS ONLY AROSE ON MEAT ON WHICH FLIES HAD LAID EGGS...

No flies on me!

Let me in!

Yum!

BZZz

*ITALY, 1626-1697.

AND IN THE 1860S, FRENCH CHEMIST LOUIS PASTEUR (1822-1895) PROVED THAT BOILED SOUP ONLY WENT OFF IF BACTERIA COULD GET INTO IT...

Clever science, but it made me very hungry!

THIS WAY OF PRESERVING FOOD IS CALLED 'PASTEURISATION'.

PEOPLE TODAY NOW ACCEPT THAT MICRO-ORGANISMS DO EXIST AND SPONTANEOUS GENERATION DOESN'T. NOT THAT THERE AREN'T STILL SOME UNRESOLVED QUESTIONS...

Do we exist, dear?

You gotta believe in yourself more.

SEE PAGES 18-19 FOR MORE MYTHICAL MONSTERS!

KINGDOM 3: Protozoa

🌐 Over 50,000 species ☆ Sheer variety

Protozoa ('PRO-TOE-ZOH-A') are a mixed bag of single-celled eukaryotic organisms that feed on bacteria, algae and organic matter. Most are small and harmless, but a few can cause diseases. Found worldwide, they live anywhere wet, including in damp soils and the insides of many animals – including humans!

Buzz off!

The disease malaria is responsible for hundreds of thousands of deaths every year, largely in hot countries. It is caused by a protozoan parasite called *Plasmodium* and is introduced when infected mosquitoes feed on human blood.

Get a move on!

Protozoa have three ways of moving through their wet worlds.

1. By spinning a spiral flagellum like a propeller

2. By flowing their bodies into arm-like extensions called 'pseudopods'

3. By beating lots of tiny hairs known as 'cilia'

Giardia lamblia is a parasite of humans and swims in your intestines using its flagella. It can cause a runny tummy and eggy-smelling burps.

Amoeba proteus lives in ponds and moves by flowing its body into a series of pseudopods. It engulfs particles of food.

Paramecium caudatum moves through water by beating the many thousands of cilia covering its body, though only one-third of a millimetre in length.

🔍 SIGNS OF LIFE:

☐ SOILS
☐ SEAS
☐ RIVERS
☐ YOU!

KINGDOM 4: Chromista

🌐 Over 180,000 species ☆ Photosynthesis

This is another mixed group whose members mostly live in water. They photosynthesise like plants, but with a different form of chlorophyll (see page 21). The group includes tiny marine organisms called 'diatoms' and some giant brown seaweeds. The name 'chromista' ('KROH-MISS-TA') comes from the colourful pigments many contain, though some are completely colourless.

Kelp is harvested to make alginate, a gum used to thicken foods, including ice cream. Look for the name, or the food additive numbers E400, E401 and E402.

diatoms

Small but perfectly formed

Diatoms are microscopic but have beautiful glass-like shells and are an important food for marine plankton.

Fronds for life

The largest chromista are brown seaweeds, such as giant kelp. Growing up to 50 metres long, kelp forms huge underwater forests in temperate (cool) oceans. These are home to sea otters, who wrap themselves in kelp so they don't float away while they sleep!

🔍 SIGNS OF LIFE:

☐ OCEANS
☐ SEAS
☐ ROCKPOOLS
☐ ICE CREAM!

lamina

holdfast

LIFE STORIES

ROUND ABOUT THE MIDDLE AGES*, BIOLOGY WENT BONKERS...

I am off to catch ye dragon, or perhaps ye griffin or ye basilisk.

Just ye rabbit would do...

*THE 5ᵀᴴ–15ᵀᴴ CENTURIES CE.

MONKS MIXED MYTHS WITH RELIGION TO PRODUCE BEAUTIFUL BOOKS OF MARVELLOUSLY MAD ANIMALS...

This one I'm drawing is half man, half donkey... and half serpent.

Sounds like a beast-and-a-half to me!

THE BOOKS BELONGED TO SUPER-RICH NOBLES.

THESE HIGHLY ILLUSTRATED MANUSCRIPTS WERE DEVELOPED FROM THE WRITINGS OF THE ANCIENT ROMANS AND GREEKS – NOT ALL OF THEM ACCURATE.

Me, Aristotle, again. Sorry about that...

BECAUSE THEY MOSTLY DESCRIBED ANIMALS ('BEASTS'), THEY WERE CALLED 'BESTIARIES'. MANY WERE REALLY WEIRD...

BASILISK
Kills by hissing.

JACULUS
Winged snake that loiters in trees.

GRIFFIN
Body of a lion, head of an eagle, hunts horses.

BONNACON
Blasts dung from its rump in defence.

AMPHISBAENA
Head at both ends.

MANTICORE
Human head, lion's body, scorpion tail. Oh, and blue eyes.

BESTIARIES ALSO INCLUDED THE ODD (OFTEN VERY ODD) PLANT, SUCH AS THE MANDRAKE... THE MANDRAKE ROOT IS SHAPED LIKE A NAKED HUMAN. IT SHRIEKS WHEN DUG UP, AND HEARING IT MEANS DEATH. THAT ASIDE, IT'S SAID TO BE DELICIOUS.

This is so embarrassing. No wonder we scream.

SOME BEASTS MAY HAVE HAD A BASIS IN FACT... FOR EXAMPLE, DINOSAUR FOSSILS ARE THOUGHT TO HAVE INSPIRED STORIES OF DRAGONS*.

I dig dragons – for real!

*CHINA IS STILL HOME TO MANY NEW DINO FOSSIL FINDS.

PEOPLE ALSO FAKED EVIDENCE FOR BEASTS IN THE BESTIARIES. FOR EXAMPLE, TUSKS OF THE NARWHAL – A MARINE MAMMAL – WERE SAID TO COME FROM UNICORNS...

ITS TUSK IS ACTUALLY AN OVERGROWN TOOTH.

ANOTHER MARINE MAMMAL – THE MANATEE – IS SAID TO HAVE INSPIRED STORIES OF MERMAIDS WHEN SAILORS SAW THEM SUNBATHING ON ROCKS...

MERMAIDS PROVED SO POPULAR THAT CLEVER CONMEN MADE FAKE MERMAIDS USING PARTS FROM STUFFED ANIMALS...

MANY MAJOR SCIENCE MUSEUMS OWN ONE OF THESE FAKES!

BUT EVEN WHEN REAL ANIMALS FEATURED IN BESTIARIES, THE SO-CALLED FACTS WERE OFTEN FICTION...

VERY OCCASIONALLY, BESTIARIES CONTAINED SOME AMAZING CLAIMS THAT WERE ACTUALLY TRUE...

...BUT NOBODY BELIEVED THEM!

SCIENTISTS PUT THEIR FAITH IN BESTIARIES FOR MANY CENTURIES*, AND – DESPITE BEING BONKERS – THEY STILL FEATURE IN OUR CULTURE TODAY...

*SEE PAGE 30.

KINGDOM 5: Planta

🌍 Over 390,000 species

☆ Turning light into life

The study of plants is called botany, and botanists know that all plants are wonderful – even weeds! Without plants, pretty much all life on Earth would cease to exist.

Plants sit at the bottom of a pyramid of living things known as a food chain. Plants grow and get eaten by animals, passing on their energy. Other animals eat those animals. When all these organisms eventually die, they are eaten and decomposed by bacteria, fungi and yet more animals. Eventually, this energy returns to nature and the whole process goes around again!

Plant power

Plants are plentiful! They make up 80% of the total mass of life on Earth and are found on every continent, including Antarctica. All animals – including humans – rely, ultimately, on plants. Plants feed us, clothe us and provide the materials for tools, shelter and medicines. Plants also produce the oxygen we need to breathe, and take harmful carbon from the atmosphere so it can't contribute to climate change.

Plants are also incredible invaders! They colonise newly exposed areas on Earth to form brand-new habitats, allowing other organisms to follow. Different plants produce different habitats, resulting in the huge variety of living things to be found on Earth – an idea known as 'biodiversity'.

Plants deserve our thanks. Maybe we should send them some flowers!

Light fantastic

Photosynthesis is how plants trap the energy in sunlight to make their own food. Special organelles called 'chloroplasts' in the cells of leaves use this energy to combine carbon dioxide (CO_2) from the air with water (H_2O) from their environment to produce sugars and oxygen (O_2). The oxygen is released into the air and the sugars are used to feed the plant and build new cells.

Chloroplasts contain a pigment called 'chlorophyll'. This absorbs only red and blue light, and reflects green light, which is why plants appear green!

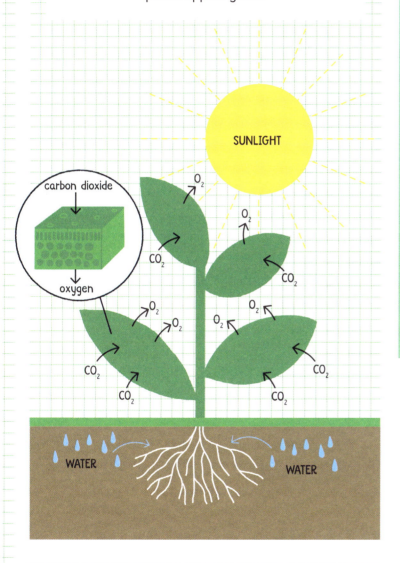

Leafy lunch

Not keen on greens? A meaty fast-food feast is ultimately entirely due to plants. Sadly, it still doesn't count towards your five a day. And, of course, there will be bacteria too!

BUN
made from plants

RELISH
made from plants

CHEESE
milk made from cows eating plants

PATTY
meat from cows fed on plants

MILK SHAKE
made from cows fed on plants

FRIES
made from plants

SUGAR
made from plants

CARTON
made from plants

The green scene

Plants have been around for over 500 million years. Today, they range from tiny single-celled green algae (see page 22) to giant trees such as redwoods (see page 25) that are among the heaviest living things on the planet. Some are poisonous, some are pretty and some are pretty strange!

Venus fly-trap — eats insects!

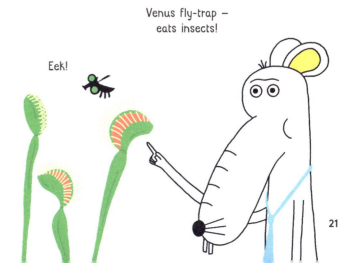

Eek!

🧪 Shine on

You can show photosynthesis at home by submerging some fresh watercress or spinach in cold water. Shine a strong light on the leaves and small bubbles of oxygen should eventually appear.

Lower Plants: Green for 'Go'

The first plants were simple little things, without roots, leaves, seeds or flowers. Some stayed in the water, others took a giant evolutionary leap and invaded the land. They grew at the edges of lakes and rivers, and many of their modern descendants still need water, or wet spots, to survive. Here we say 'hi' to these so-called lower plants.

Green algae

🌐 About 8,000 species

Mostly aquatic, green algae ('AL-GEE') species range from single cells to the 30 centimetre-wide blades of sea lettuce (*Ulva lactuca*). Sea lettuce can wash up on beaches in vast amounts, where it rots, releasing hydrogen sulphide, a toxic gas smelling of bad eggs.

Harmless freshwater algae often grow inside pets' water bottles that are exposed to light. *Chlorella*, a single-celled alga that clouds the sides of fish tanks, is a superfood and is now being mass-produced for humans as it is high in protein.

Volvox, a green alga found in ponds, forms beautiful colonies of thousands of cells, with daughter colonies inside them. Colonies can be 2 millimetres across and will move towards a bright light.

Cooksonia, one of the very first land plants – 400 million years ago. (Now extinct.)

volvox

🔍 SIGNS OF LIFE:

☐ ANYWHERE WET

☐ HEALTH-FOOD SHOPS

Bryophytes

🌐 About 12,000 species

Bryophytes are the distant descendants of those pioneering plants that first invaded the land. Today, the group includes hornworts, liverworts and mosses, and can be found all over the world, from Arctic wastes to deserts and rainforests.

Hornworts get their name from a reproductive structure that grows upwards and looks like a horn, while 'wort' is just an old English word meaning 'small plant'.

Many liverworts have a flat green body (called a 'thallus') with lobes that give them their common name. Because they look like a human liver, ancient people thought they cured liver diseases.

Mosses love moisture. *Sphagnum* moss grows in huge bogs and is harvested as peat and used to improve soils, or it is dried and burned.

Because dry *Sphagnum* is highly absorbent, native Americans also used it in babies' nappies. It can hold twenty times its weight in water!

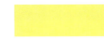

🔎 SIGNS OF LIFE:

☐ GARDEN PEAT

Lycophytes

🌐 About 1,290 species

Lycophytes ('LIKE-O-FITES') are an odd mix of plants including quillworts and so-called clubmosses.

Clubmosses are not true mosses. 300 million years ago, their ancestors were giant trees 40 metres tall whose remains form much of the coal we mine today. The stag's-horn clubmoss (*Lycopodium clavatum*) grows just 15 centimetres tall but produces clouds of tiny spores (reproductive units a little like seeds) that explode if ignited, and which were once added to fireworks or used for make-up.

Selaginella, the so-called resurrection plant, is a Mexican lycophyte that can survive for years as a dry, brown ball. It unfolds back to bright green life within hours of being given water, and can be bought as a botanical novelty.

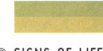

🔎 SIGNS OF LIFE:

☐ COAL
☐ PLANT SHOPS

Pteridophytes

🌐 About 12,000 species

Pteridophytes ('TEH-REE-DO-FITES') include ferns and the bristly horsetails, whose ancestors grew as tall as trees back in the Carboniferous period.

In Victorian times, people went fern-crazy, collecting wild ferns to keep at home and decorating all manner of items with their image. Even today, the British 'custard cream' biscuit has a fern-pattern decoration. As a result of over-collecting, some species became extinct.

CUSTARD CREAM

Horsetails got their common name for obvious reasons. Their scientific name is *Equisetum*, which means 'horse bristle'. Horsetail stems are reinforced with abrasive silica – a glass-like mineral – and were once used to scour metal pots.

🔎 SIGNS OF LIFE:

☐ WOODS AND WATERSIDES
☐ FIELDS AND FORESTS
☐ BISCUIT BARREL

Gymnosperms: Seeds of Change

🌐 Over 1,000 known species

Gymnosperms ('JIM-NO-SPERMS') is the scientific name for a very familiar group of plants that includes the traditional Christmas tree.

Gymnosperms differ from so-called lower plants in having roots, true leaves and special tissues for transporting nutrients and water. However, most significantly for biologists, they produce seeds.

Seeds contain tiny embryonic versions of their parent plants, ready to sprout and grow if conditions are right. Seed-producing plants fall into two groups – Angiosperms (see page 28) and Gymnosperms – and make up the majority of known plant species on Earth, including our most important food crops.

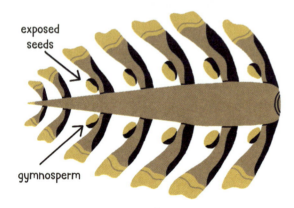

exposed seeds

gymnosperm

pine cone

Gymnosperm means 'naked seed' – referring to the open way in which their seeds develop, often inside a cone.

Gymnosperms are divided into four major groups: cycads, ginkgo, gnetales and conifers. The world needs seeds!

Cycads

🌐 Over 300 species

Some cycads ('SY-KADS') look like palm trees, others like pineapples. In fact, they are an ancient group of plants whose ancestors also contributed to the coal we burn so casually. One cycad – the misleadingly named sago palm – has a starchy pith that can be cooked and eaten and was once a staple of stodgy school dinners!

sago pudding

Ginkgo

🌐 Just one species

Known from fossils 270 million years old, this group has just one surviving species, *Ginkgo biloba*. It is common in parks worldwide, but in the wild is found only in China, where its distinctive leaves are used in traditional medicine and its seeds eaten as a delicacy. It's amazingly hardy: four ginkgo trees survived the atomic bomb dropped on Hiroshima, Japan, in 1945, despite being only 1.5 kilometres from the blast.

The ginkgo leaf is now the emblem of Tokyo.

Gnetales

🌐 About 90 species

The group Gnetales ('NET-ALES') includes a weird but wonderful plant called *Welwitschia mirabilis* that lives in dry deserts in Africa. It produces just two leathery leaves that become scruffily torn and twisted with age, but which serve to drip fog on to its roots at night. Utterly unique, it is the national plant of Namibia – a Commonwealth country – and was depicted on the wedding dress of Meghan Markle.

Conifers

🌐 Over 600 species

'Conifer' means 'cone-bearing'. Cones come in many shapes and sizes, as do the trees that carry them. Male cones develop first and release pollen that fertilises the female cones, where the seeds form. Many conifers are 'evergreen', meaning they keep their leaves all year round.

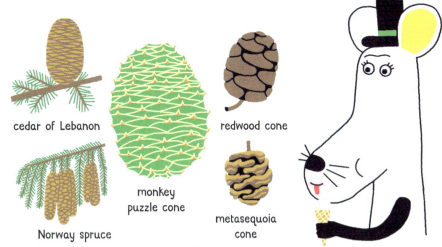

cedar of Lebanon

Norway spruce

monkey puzzle cone

redwood cone

metasequoia cone

The world's oldest living tree grows at a secret location in California. It is a bristlecone pine and is more than 5,000 years old, meaning that it pre-dates the pyramids.

Amber – the fossilised sap of prehistoric pine trees – can hold the preserved remains of life long gone.

The USA is home to many trunk-tastic trees. At over 115 metres, 'Hyperion', a coast redwood growing in California, is currently the world's tallest, and would tower over the Statue of Liberty.

The Chilean pine is commonly called the monkey puzzle because its spiky branches would perplex any monkey looking to climb them. Properly named *Araucaria*, these trees date back to the time of dinosaurs and their fossilised wood forms the mineral jet, used for jet-black jewellery.

Humans rely on conifers. We eat their seeds (pine nuts) and use their sticky sap for perfumes. The wood from firs and spruces – known as softwood – is harvested for building and making furniture, as well as the paper and card of this book you are reading!

very tall

Where exactly is it growing? I'm not at liberty to say!

🔎 SIGNS OF LIFE:

- ☐ BUILDINGS
- ☐ FURNITURE
- ☐ BOOKS
- ☐ PAPER
- ☐ PINE NUTS
- ☐ CHRISTMAS TREES

LIFE STORIES

STUDYING PLANTS GOES BACK TO THE START OF FARMING MORE THAN 10,000 YEARS AGO...

Are you an early farmer?

No, I prefer a lie-in.

THE MIDDLE EAST, c.11,000 BCE

AS WELL AS CROPS, SOME PLANTS WERE ALSO VALUABLE MEDICINES...

Take this, three times a day.

Before or after meals?

CHINA, c.2,600 BCE

HOWEVER, SOME PLANTS KILLED RATHER THAN CURED...

You're green!

I've eaten too many leaves. URK!

NEVER EAT PLANTS THAT YOU DON'T KNOW ARE SAFE!

THEOPHRASTUS PLACED PLANTS IN FOUR GROUPS, THE FIRST ATTEMPT AT THEIR CLASSIFICATION...

TREES

What do you think of my system?

It's growing on me.

HERBS

SHRUBS

UNDERSHRUBS

THEOPHRASTUS STUDIED PLANTS IN GREAT DETAIL AND IDENTIFIED MORE THAN 500 DIFFERENT TYPES...

Including asparagus. Yum!

ENQUIRIES INTO PLANTS

CAUSES OF PLANTS

HIS BOOKS REMAINED THE BEST ON BOTANY FOR ALMOST 2,000 YEARS.

PEOPLE EVEN CREATED SPECIAL GARDENS* TO GROW THE HEALING PLANTS – THE ORIGINS OF TODAY'S BOTANIC GARDENS...

This one cures backache.

I hope so... Ouch!

*CALLED 'PHYSIC' GARDENS, AFTER AN OLD WORD FOR 'MEDICINE'.

LOST FOR 1,800 YEARS, THEOPHRASTUS'S WORKS FINALLY RESURFACED. THEY INSPIRED ITALIAN BOTANIST ANDREA CESALPINO WHO, IN 1583, PUBLISHED A RATHER UNUSUAL PLANT BOOK.

No pictures!

Pity!

BUT IT WAS THE FIRST TO CLASSIFY PLANTS BY THEIR FLOWERS, FRUITS AND SEEDS.

CESALPINO WAS ALSO ONE OF THE FIRST BOTANISTS TO MAKE A HERBARIUM – A COLLECTION OF DRIED PRESSED PLANTS ON PAPER.

I'm working flat out!

SEE OPPOSITE FOR HOW TO MAKE YOUR OWN.

HERBARIUMS WERE USED TO CREATE NEW BOOKS SHOWING ALL KNOWN PLANTS, NOT JUST MEDICINAL ONES. SUCH A BOOK WAS CALLED A 'FLORA'.

Like my flora, Flora?

Lovely, Dudley!

THEY GROUPED TOGETHER SIMILAR PLANTS AND HELPED IDENTIFY ALREADY KNOWN SPECIES.

PLANT HUNTERS OFTEN RISKED THEIR LIVES TO COLLECT SPECIMENS FOR MUSEUMS AND UNIVERSITIES...

If I get this home, they better name it after me...

SEVEN STUDENTS DIED WHILE COLLECTING PLANTS FOR THE SWEDISH BOTANIST CARL LINNAEUS (SEE PAGE 30).

UNLIKE OTHER SCIENCES, BOTANY WAS CONSIDERED SUITABLE FOR WOMEN... IN COLONIAL AMERICA, JANE COLDEN* RECORDED THE PLANTS GROWING WILD IN NEW YORK STATE.

Just as well – it's mostly concrete.

*UNITED STATES, 1724–1766

THE CASE OF THE BLOOMING BRILLIANT BOTANISTS

5

RST, PEOPLE STUDIED ONLY
UL' PLANTS, BUT ONE PERSON
GHT DIFFERENTLY...

Me again, folks.

NOT ARISTOTLE (SEE PAGE 13)...

...BUT HIS PUPIL AND CLOSE FRIEND THEOPHRASTUS* – KNOWN TODAY AS THE 'FATHER OF BOTANY'...

My turn!

Hmmph!

*GREECE, c.372–287 BCE

AFTER HE DIED, HIS WRITINGS
LOST. ATTENTION RETURNED TO
CINAL PLANTS, AND THE WRITINGS
HE GREEK DOCTOR DIOSCORIDES*,
WORKED FOR THE ROMAN ARMY.

ke this, three
nes a day.

Before or
after battles?

EECE, c.40–90 CE

DIOSCORIDES, AND OTHERS WHO CAME AFTER HIM, PRODUCED BEAUTIFULLY ILLUSTRATED BOOKS OF HEALING PLANTS...

Will this make me better?

No – but isn't
it pretty?

KNOWN AS 'HERBALS', THESE BOOKS DESCRIBED THOUSANDS OF SPECIES BY THE SIXTEENTH CENTURY.

NISTS HUNTED OUT NEW PLANTS TO DESCRIBE. WHEN THE ENGLISH SCIENTIST
RAY* FINISHED HIS *HISTORIA PLANTARUM* IN 1704, IT CONTAINED MORE THAN
0 SPECIES FROM AS FAR AWAY AS JAMAICA. RAY ALSO COINED THE TERM 'PETAL'...

fore me, they
ere called
oloured leaves'!

Well done, petal!

GLAND, 1627–1705

WOMEN WERE ALSO WONDERS WHEN
ME TO BOTANICAL ILLUSTRATION.
ISHWOMAN MARIANNE NORTH*
ELLED SOLO OVER THE GLOBE
TING WILD PLANTS...

least they
ep still.

HER PICTURES AT THE ROYAL
NIC GARDENS, KEW, LONDON.
0–1890

OVER 2,000 YEARS ON FROM THEOPHRASTUS, BRAVE BOTANISTS STILL SEARCH OUT NEW PLANT SPECIES BEFORE THEY ARE LOST FOREVER – PLANTS THAT COULD GIVE US NEW FOODS OR MEDICINES.

SAVE THE SPECIES!

KINGDOM 5: PLANTA

🧪 Under pressure

You can try preserving plant specimens from the garden by pressing them. Collect whole small plants or just selected parts. Avoid using wet specimens and shake off any soil.

Lay out your specimen on some sheets of clean kitchen roll. Add more on top, with several sheets of newspaper above and below.

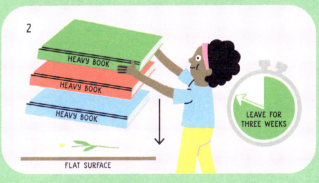

HEAVY BOOK

HEAVY BOOK

HEAVY BOOK

FLAT SURFACE

LEAVE FOR
THREE WEEKS

Then place the whole thing on a flat surface with a pile of heavy books on top. Leave for a few weeks while the paper absorbs the moisture from the plant.

Remove the dry, flat specimen, then glue it carefully on to a clean sheet of paper, and label it.

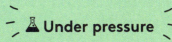

Angiosperms: Flower Power

🌐 Over 350,000 species

Angiosperms ('AN-JEE-OH-SPERMS') are flowering plants. They dominate the land and provide a dazzlingly diverse array of habitats for other living things. Without them, human life would be practically impossible. All our important food crops are angiosperms – from bananas to potatoes, wheat to rice. We rely on them for shelter, clothing, chemicals, materials, medicines and so much more. They also delight us with their scent and beauty. Flowering plants are blooming brilliant!

Pollen counts!

Angiosperms use flowers to reproduce sexually. The male parts produce pollen which fertilise the female parts, leading to seeds forming inside a fruit or pod. (The name 'angiosperm' means 'cased seed'.) Some flowers self-pollinate, some spread their pollen to other individuals, often tricking animals into doing it for them!

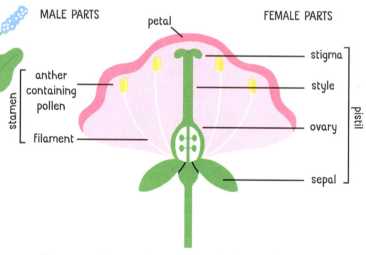

MALE PARTS

petal

FEMALE PARTS

stamen
- anther containing pollen
- filament

- stigma
- style
- ovary
- sepal

pistil

Every species produces uniquely shaped grains of pollen which, despite their tiny size, can be very intricate and beautiful.

hazel pollen

willow pollen
(magnified about 500 times)

rose pollen

Hives of activity

Flowers first appear in the fossil record about 160 million years ago, a very long time before bees. The first flowers were probably pollinated by beetles coming to munch on their pollen and accidentally spreading it to other plants. Modern magnolias are very like these ancient flowers and today still bloom early in the year, well before bees wake up from winter.

Bees are top pollinators because their hairy bodies pick up pollen. Whether they go solo or live in colonies, like honeybees, they visit flowers for the protein in pollen and the energy in sugary sweet nectar. Back in the hive, honeybees pass nectar mouth-to-mouth to turn it into honey. Over 100 top crops are pollinated by these invaluable insects, which is why we need to keep bees buzzing!

blueberries

almonds

apples

honey

While humans admire flowers for their beauty, bees see so much more. Bees can register ultraviolet light (invisible to humans), revealing special nectar guides leading them down to a sticky, sweet treat.

WE SEE

BEES SEE

Bee orchids have a cunning plan when it comes to pollination, producing a flower that mimics a female bumblebee. Real male bees attempt to mate with it, spreading pollen in the process.

Many trees, and most grasses including wheat and bamboo, use the wind and rain to carry their pollen. In some susceptible humans, this causes hay fever: sneezing, a runny nose and irritated eyes.

Flower tower

'Centurion', the nickname of a eucalyptus tree in a secret location in Tasmania, is the world's tallest flowering plant. At 100.5 metres it is the only plant over 100 metres tall outside California.

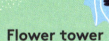

Dead smelly

The world's largest flower belongs to *Rafflesia arnoldii*, a parasitic plant found in Sumatran forests. Known as the stinking corpse flower, the 30 centimetre-wide flower reeks of rancid rotting flesh and attracts hundreds of hungry flies, which carry off its pollen.

Nectar detectors

The largest wild pollinator is the black-and-white ruffed lemur of Madagascar. This pollinates the traveller's tree (*Ravenala*) while feasting on hard-to-get nectar. *Ravenala* is also the only plant in the world with blue seeds!

Plants can also be pollinated by hummingbirds, hawkmoths and bats.

Hummingbirds rely on the energy in nectar to keep flying, and can visit over 1,000 flowers a day!

One orchid growing in Madagascar is pollinated by a moth with a 28 centimetre-long tongue!

The agave cactus of Mexico is pollinated by bats that drink nectar at night.

🔍 SIGNS OF LIFE:

☐ PRETTY MUCH EVERYWHERE

☐ BEGIN WITH THE FRUIT BOWL!

LIFE STORIES

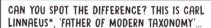

CAN YOU SPOT THE DIFFERENCE? THIS IS CARL LINNAEUS*, 'FATHER OF MODERN TAXONOMY'...

Hi!

*SWEDEN, 1707–1778

...AND THIS IS CARL VON LINNÉ*, 'PRINCE OF BOTANISTS'.

Hi, again!

*SWEDEN, 1707–1778

SAME PERSON EACH TIME, BUT TWO DIFFERENT NAME

Just call me Carl, oka

LIVING THINGS MAY ALSO HAVE MORE THAN ONE NAME, MAKING LIFE VERY CONFUSING.

TO AVOID THIS PROBLEM, SCIENCE NEEDED A SHORT, UNIQUE NAME FOR EVERY ORGANISM – A PROBLEM LINNAEUS SET OUT TO SOLVE...

And I succeeded!

HE DID!

THANKS TO LINNAEUS, THE WILD ROSE NOW HAS ONE NAME USED BY SCIENTISTS EVERYWHERE...

Rosa canina **L.**

I preferred 'Fred'.

THE L. SHOWS IT WAS NAMED BY LINNAEUS.

HOW DID THIS HAPPEN? WELL, LINNAEUS TRAINED ORIGINALLY AS A DOCTOR, BUT HIS REAL PASSION WAS FOR PLANTS...

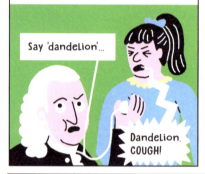

Say 'dandelion'...

Dandelion. COUGH!

SINCE CHILDHOOD, HE HAD STUDIED PLANTS FROM ALL OVER THE WORLD AND, ONE DAY, HE HIT ON A NEW WAY OF ORGANISING THEM...

IDEA

'FLOWER–BULB MOMENT!'

WITHIN A GENUS, EXTRA DIFFERENCES INDICATED A DIFFERENT SPECIES.

Smells good!

Rosa canina, unscented

Rosa rugosa, scented

(ROSE SPECIES MAY ALSO DIFFER IN WAYS OTHER THAN SCENT.)

USING LINNAEUS'S SYSTEM, EVERY ORGANISM – NOT JUST PLANTS – COULD BE GIVEN A TWO–PART SCIENTIFIC NAME OF GENUS AND SPECIES...

I call this binomial nomenclature!

Hmm, I'm in two minds about it...

BUT THOUGH LINNAEUS WAS SUPER–SCIENTIFIC, HIS SYSTEM ALSO INCLUDED SOME FANTASTIC BEASTS SUCH AS THE MANTICORE AND UNICORN...

Just in case they <u>did</u> exist...

You mean we don't?

MEDIEVAL BESTIARIES STILL HAD AN INFLUENCE (SEE PAGES 18–19).

LINNAEUS'S BOOK WAS A HIT, AND EACH NEW EDITION ADDED YET MORE SPECIES, INCLUDING HUMANS.

I put us in with the apes.

You must be bananas!

THIS WAS HUGELY CONTROVERSIAL, ESPECIALLY BECAUSE LINNAEUS HIMSELF BELIEVED IN CREATION AND THE GREAT CHAIN OF BEING*, PLACING HUMANS ABOVE NATURE...

My fault! Sorr

*SEE PAGE 13.

... EXAMPLE, ELIZABETHAN COUNTRY CALLED THE WILD ROSE MANY [THIN]GS...

...og rose!

Cock-bramble!

...glantine!

Fred!

WHILE BOTANISTS AT THE TIME GAVE IT LONG-WINDED NAMES IN LATIN*...

It's a *Rosa sylvestris inodora seu canina!*

No! It's a *Rosa sylvestris alba cum rubore folio glabro!*

*LATIN WAS THE LANGUAGE USED IN UNIVERSITIES.

[LINN]AEUS EXAMINED THEIR FLOWERS AND PUT PLANTS WITH IDENTICAL PARTS INTO [THE] SAME GROUP.

I called that group a 'genus' – and I called myself a 'genius'!

[THE] WILD ROSE IS IN THE GENUS *ROSA*.

[LINN]AEUS PUBLISHED HIS NEW 'SYSTEM OF NATURE' IN 1735. HE DIVIDED NATURE INTO [THREE] KINGDOMS...

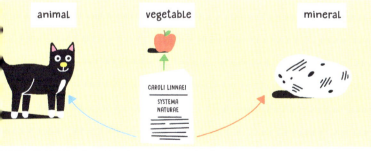

animal   vegetable   mineral

CAROLI LINNAEI
SYSTEMA NATURAE

[THE S]AME NAMES WE USE IN A GUESSING GAME TODAY!

[LINN]AEUS WROTE MANY MORE BOOKS [EXPA]NDING HIS SYSTEM, AND BECAME [THE W]ORLD'S TOP BIOLOGIST – AS WELL [AS A] BIT OF A BIG HEAD...

'God created, Linnaeus [?]organised,' as I like to [t]ell people.

I still think he's bananas.

LINNAEUS CHANGED HIS NAME TO VON LINNÉ WHEN HONOURED BY THE KING OF SWEDEN IN 1761. HIS COAT OF ARMS INCLUDED HIS FAVOURITE FLOWER...

Named after me, of course!

Linnaea borealis

KINGDOM 5: PLANTA

The name game

The tradition of naming a new species after a naturalist continues today, especially if that person was the first to find it. However, some species also get named after pop stars, presidents, film legends and many more.

Because the Earth is home to so many different insects, new species are discovered almost daily. This has given biologists a great opportunity to honour – or perhaps mock – many famous people. Here are just a few examples...

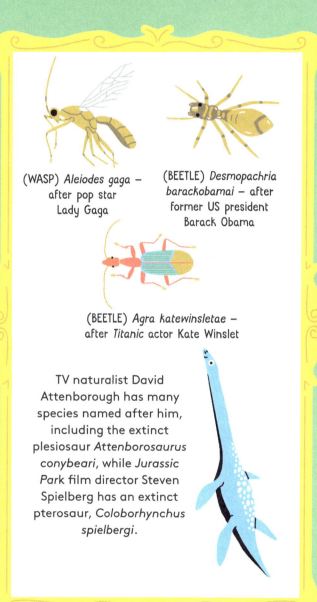

(WASP) *Aleiodes gaga* – after pop star Lady Gaga

(BEETLE) *Desmopachria barackobamai* – after former US president Barack Obama

(BEETLE) *Agra katewinsletae* – after *Titanic* actor Kate Winslet

TV naturalist David Attenborough has many species named after him, including the extinct plesiosaur *Attenborosaurus conybeari*, while *Jurassic Park* film director Steven Spielberg has an extinct pterosaur, *Coloborhynchus spielbergi*.

What creature would you want named after YOU?

KINGDOM 6: Fungi

🌐 120,000 known species, but possibly over 5 million

☆ Super-recyclers

Fungi are furtive. They exist almost everywhere but go largely unnoticed. Mostly microscopic, they are said to make up one quarter of the weight of all life on Earth.

Some fungi produce the fruiting bodies we know as mushrooms and toadstools, but the group also includes rusts, smuts, moulds, mildews, jelly fungi and yeasts.

rusts

smuts

jelly fungi

fungi

moulds

Fungi get their energy from breaking down organic material, living or dead – a process known as decomposition or rotting. This releases vital nutrients for other organisms to use, making fungi nature's number one recyclers.

Fun fungi

Mushrooms and toadstools vary widely. Many resemble odd body parts, while some look like they are straight from science fiction. All these entertaining oddities *are*, however, found on Earth.

fly agaric

giant puffball

dead man's fingers

brain mushroom

smooth cage fungus

stinkhorn fungus

night-light mushroom (glows in the dark!)

bleeding tooth fungus

Fridge fungi

Harmless yeast fungi produce the carbon dioxide gas that makes bread rise and drinks fizzy. Cooking kills the yeast in bread, and it is removed from beers and wines. Other fungi are used to produce smelly cheeses such as Camembert and Brie, and blue cheeses like Stilton.

Food or foe?

Mushrooms and toadstools contain spores, tiny particles – a little like seeds – used to colonise new areas. Some are delicious to eat, some cause hallucinations, and some are deadly poisonous. Even experts can struggle to tell tasty species from toxic ones, so DON'T experiment!

horse mushroom, edible

deathcap, dead-ible

⚗ Draw with spores

Place a large, flat edible mushroom on a sheet of white paper with its dark, feathery gills facing down. After a few days, spores should fall from the gills, staining the paper where they land. Remove the mushroom to reveal a spore print, often used to identify different species.

Humongous fungus

The largest single organism alive on Earth today is probably a honey fungus (*Armillaria solidipes*) in a forest in Oregon, USA. One individual fungus has spread through the soil over an area the size of 1,300 football pitches, killing and consuming trees as it goes. It is also said to be over 1,800 years old.

The Wood Wide Web

Many fungi live in soils as networks of microscopic threads called hyphae ('HY-FEE'), often living in association with the roots of plants. The plants and fungi both benefit from the relationship, and some trees use this fungus-style 'Internet' to warn each other of insect attacks, drought or diseases.

Together forever

Some fungi form partnerships with photosynthetic algae, producing a combination lifeform called a lichen. Many lichens don't like pollution and will grow only where the air is clean. In the Arctic, lichens form an important food for reindeer.

🔍 SIGNS OF LIFE:

- ☐ SUPERMARKETS
- ☐ FRIDGE
- ☐ BEERS
- ☐ WINES
- ☐ CHEESES
- ☐ BREAD
- ☐ ANTIBIOTICS
- ☐ ATHLETE'S FOOT CAUSED BY A FUNGUS THAT FEEDS ON SKIN

Friendly fungi

Some fungi are incredibly helpful. Many antibiotic medicines contain substances originally found in fungi. The most famous is penicillin, discovered by the Scottish scientist Alexander Fleming in 1928. Since then, many other antibiotics have been developed from fungi, with new ones constantly needed as disease organisms develop resistance.

KINGDOM 7: Animalia

🌍 Over 1.5 million known species

☆ Munching and moving

The study of animals is called zoology. Animals are often very visible organisms, moving in a multitude of ways in, over and across the globe. They range in size from microscopic to mighty, but all are multicellular eukaryotes (see page 6) with a need to feed.

Skeleton crew

Animals divide informally into two groups: those with an internal skeleton to hold them up ('vertebrates') and those without ('invertebrates'). Invertebrate 'creepy-crawlies' make up 97% of all known animal species, and nine out of ten of them are insects (see pages 42–43). Humans are massively outnumbered!

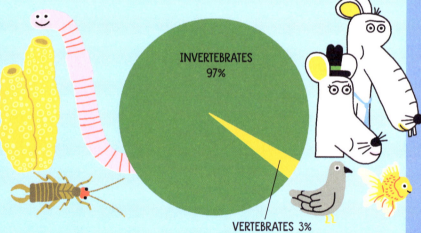

INVERTEBRATES 97%

VERTEBRATES 3%

Mirror image

Most animals–including you–are essentially tubes, where food enters at one end and wastes exit at the other. Many show bilateral symmetry, where the left and right sides of the body are mirror images. Most have a mouth. Many have their major sensory organs organised into a head at one end. Sponges, jellyfish and starfish are some exceptions and show radial symmetry, like equally slicing up a pizza.

butterfly
(bilateral symmetry)

starfish

jellyfish

(radial symmetry)

You are what you eat

Animals have evolved a vast variety of strategies for finding food–and staying alive long enough to reproduce–giving us the staggering range of species we see today. Animals that eat plants are known as 'herbivores'. Flesh-eating animals are called 'carnivores'. Animals that eat a mix of things–such as humans–are known as 'omnivores'. But, of course, in nature, nothing ever goes to waste, so there are also animals that eat such treats as poo, and dead and rotting animals and plants. These are 'scavengers' and 'detritivores'. They all have an important place in the food chain (see page 20).

elephant – herbivore

eagle – carnivore

Ohms – omnivore

dung beetle – detritivore

hyena – scavenger

34

What a nerve!

Unlike plants and fungi, the cells of animals lack rigid walls. In the 500 billion years since they first appeared, animals have evolved all sorts of cells with different functions. Most are microscopic, but if you want to know what the longest single cell in the human body is, the answer is on page 7!

nerve cell

Hot or cold

'Warm-blooded' mammals and birds are the only animals capable of maintaining a constant body temperature. All other animals are said to be 'cold-blooded' – their body temperature relies on their environment. Too cold and they cannot move or function correctly. Too hot and they die.

warm-blooded   cold-blooded

🧪 Hot to trot

Borrow a medical thermometer and take your temperature at intervals through the day. It should stay around a healthy 37°C – the best temperature for the chemical processes that take place in cells.

Little and large

The smallest animals currently known are tiny fish parasites called myxozoa. Distant cousins of sea jellies, they are just one-hundredth of a millimetre in size. In complete contrast, the blue whale is not only the largest living animal, but also the largest animal that has ever existed. The longest blue whale measured topped the tape at 33.5 metres – just pipping the dinosaur *Diplodocus*!

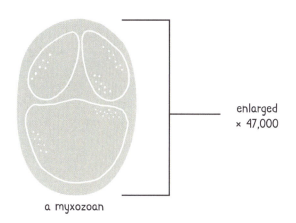

enlarged × 47,000

a myxozoan

All together now

Animal species have many different ways of getting together – or not, as the case may be! Some are loners. Giant pandas, for example, spend most of their lives solo and meet up only to mate. Birds, antelopes and fish form flocks, herds and shoals respectively, relying on safety in numbers. Insects such as bees and termites live in complex colonies where individuals work together, often with different jobs.

Human social groups are so complex that today we can even interact with people we have never met!

1 NEW MESSAGE!
From: Hattie

Scientists reckon most animal species are still to be discovered. There may be well over 7 million! :)

REPLY   DELETE

Lower Animals: Wet and Wild

The first animals arose in the oceans over 500 million years ago. Today many simpler animals still require water or wet places to live – including the moist environments inside our bodies!

Sea jellies

🌐 Over 2,000 species

Sea jellies swim by pulsing their bodies through the water, trailing stinging tentacles behind them. These fire tiny harpoons into plankton that are then moved to the mouth to be eaten: a mouth that is also the sea jelly's bottom!

🔍 SIGNS OF LIFE

- [ ] LOOK OUT FOR THEM ON THE BEACH!

Sponges

🌐 About 5,000 species

Sponges feed by pumping water through their hollow bodies, filtering out food particles. Amazingly, if you put a sponge through a blender, its cells will reform into a sponge again! The soft, springy skeletons of some sponges are used as bath sponges.

🔍 SIGNS OF LIFE:

- [ ] BATH SPONGE

Flatworms

🌐 Over 20,000 species

These simple worms have flattened bodies and can be found in ponds and damp soils. However, many are also parasites, including tapeworms that infect the intestines of pets and people.

🔍 SIGNS OF LIFE

- [ ] PONDS
- [ ] SOILS
- [ ] PETS
- [ ] PEOPLE

a typical tapeworm

Bryozoans

🌐 Over 4,000 species

These marine organisms sieve food from the water using feathery tentacles. Some species look like seaweeds or corals and are eaten by sea slugs and starfish.

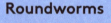

🔍 SIGNS OF LIFE:

- [ ] TROPICAL SEAS

Roundworms

🌐 Over 25,000 species

Roundworms are circular in cross-section. They exist in unimaginably huge numbers, possibly making up 80% of all individual animals on the planet.

🔍 SIGNS OF LIFE

- [ ] EVERYWHERE

Corals

🌐 Over 2,500 species

A coral is a strange 'super-animal' formed from lots of tiny identical individuals that produce a hard, chalky structure as their home. Many corals together make up a reef.

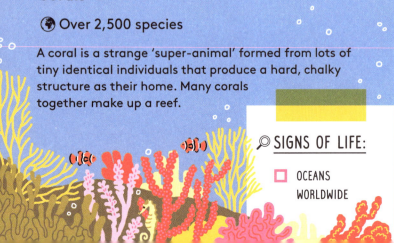

🔍 SIGNS OF LIFE:

- [ ] OCEANS WORLDWIDE

Annelid worms

🌐 Over 22,000 species

A group with three main members: ragworms that live in burrows on sandy beaches, aquatic leeches that suck blood and were once commonly used in medicine, and earthworms that live in soil and eat leaves.

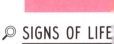

🔍 SIGNS OF LIFE

- [ ] BEACHES
- [ ] HOSPITALS
- [ ] GARDENS

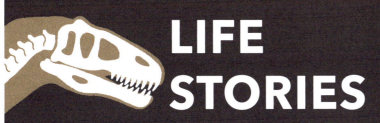

IN THE PAST, PEOPLE HAD SOME DOTTY IDEAS ABOUT FOSSILS...

A snake turned to stone by a saint.

A lightning bolt from heaven.

The devil's own toenail!

1. 2. 3.

1. AMMONITE 2. BELEMNITE 3. GRYPHAEA

FISH FOSSILS FOUND ON MOUNTAINSIDES WERE SAID TO BE EVIDENCE OF THE BIBLE STORY OF NOAH'S FLOOD...

The Flood left them high and dry...

Sounds a bit wet to me...

THEY DIDN'T REALISE THE EARTH'S CRUST FOLDS TO FORM MOUNTAINS, EXPOSING ANCIENT SEABEDS.

THE FRENCH ZOOLOGIST GEORGES CUVIER* COMPARED FOSSIL ANIMALS TO THEIR LIVING LOOKALIKES AND CAME UP WITH AN AMAZING IDEA...

mammoth, dead.

elephant, alive.

Some species that once existed are no longer around!

CUVIER (*FRANCE, 1769–1832) HAD HIT ON 'EXTINCTION' – THE END OF A SPECIES.

CLEVER CUVIER ALSO REALISED THAT, THOUGH MAMMALS WERE NOW 'TOP DOG', SO TO SPEAK, BEFORE THEM OTHER ANIMALS HAD RULED THE EARTH...

I suggested an Age of Reptiles...

Those were the days.

CUVIER IDENTIFIED THE FIRST PTEROSAUR FOSSIL AND THE FIRST MOSASAUR.

GEOLOGISTS SAW SIMILAR CHANGES IN THE FOSSILS IN SUCCESSIVE LAYERS OF ROCKS. SIMPLER ORGANISMS WERE USUALLY IN THE LOWER – OLDER – LAYERS...

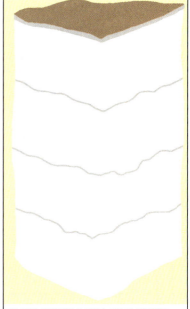

FOSSILS PROVIDE USEFUL CLUES TO THE AGES OF ROCKS.

FURTHER EVIDENCE OF LONG-LOST LIFE CAME FROM THE FINDS OF FAMOUS FOSSIL HUNTERS...

DINO- SAUR

MARY ANNING (UK, 1799–1847) FOUND THE FIRST ICHTHYOSAUR (A MARINE REPTILE) AND THE FIRST DINOSAUR POOS ('COPROLITES')!

WILLIAM BUCKLAND (UK, 1784–1856) DESCRIBED THE FIRST DINO, MEGALOSAURUS, IN 1824 – 18 YEARS BEFORE THE WORD 'DINOSAUR' WAS INVENTED.

GIDEON MANTELL (UK, 1790–1852) IDENTIFIED THE SECOND DINOSAUR, IGUANODON, A GIANT PLANT EATER, IN 1825.

RICHARD OWEN (UK, 1804–1892) CAME UP WITH THE WORD 'DINOSAUR' (MEANING 'TERRIBLE LIZARD') IN 1842. BUT ARGUED WITH DARWIN ABOUT EVOLUTION (SEE PAGES 44–45).

CUVIER SET ABOUT PLACING PREHISTORIC ORGANISMS INTO CARL LINNAEUS'S SUPER NEW SYSTEM (SEE PAGES 30–31).

You two, you're in the class Reptilia...

Welcome to the gang!

HOWEVER, CUVIER ALSO HAD SOME DOTTY IDEAS ABOUT FOSSILS. HE CLAIMED NEW SPECIES – SOMEHOW – SIMPLY APPEARED AFTER OTHERS WENT EXTINCT, REFUSING TO BELIEVE THEY MIGHT COME FROM CHANGES IN EXISTING SPECIES*...

They never change!

Just like you, eh?

*THE THEORY OF EVOLUTION (SEE PAGE 45).

TO BE FAIR, CUVIER HADN'T SEEN ANY EVIDENCE. THEN, IN 1861, A FOSSIL WAS FOUND IN GERMANY WITH A BEAK AND FEATHERS LIKE A BIRD, BUT TEETH LIKE A REPTILE...

ARCHAEOPTERYX: PART BIRD, PART DINO – IT IS CALLED A 'TRANSITIONAL' FOSSIL.

THERE WERE HUGE BATTLES AHEAD ABOUT HOW NEW SPECIES AROSE. BUT CUVIER WOULDN'T SEE THEM. HE DIED IN PARIS, IN 1832, WELL BEFORE THE STORM OF THE 'EVOLUTION REVOLUTION'...

Now, I too am extinct. Au revoir!

Molluscs and Echinoderms: Shells, Pearls, Slime and Spines

These are two more groups of animals that rate water as wonderful! Molluscs include slugs, snails and octopuses, and its members can be found in damp places on land as well as in the water. Echinoderms is a group that includes starfish and sea urchins, all of which make the oceans their home.

Molluscs

Molluscs date back to the coiled ammonites (see page 37) found as fossils – and even earlier. There are some odd minor members of this group, but molluscs are usually divided into three main gangs: gastropods, bivalves and cephalopods.

sea slug

nautilus

clam

snail

octopus

🧪 **Snail trail**

Find some garden snails hiding in a damp spot during the day. Mark their shells with a dot of nail varnish, then check again the next day. Have they come back or might they have been eaten by a hungry hedgehog?

Gastropods

🌐 About 65,000 species

The name 'gastropod' means 'stomach–foot', and this massive group of molluscs has invaded almost every environment going – much to the annoyance of many gardeners, as it includes slugs and snails!

Snails show some classic features shared by many other molluscs. They have soft bodies that are kept firm by water being under pressure inside them. This is known as a 'hydrostatic skeleton'. They also have a ribbon-like toothed tongue called a 'radula' for grinding up their food – including our precious plants!

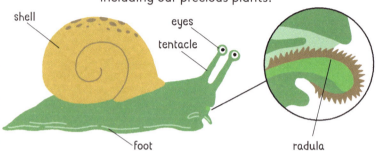

shell

eyes

tentacle

foot

radula

Some gastropods have amazing homing instincts. When marine limpets spend time above water, they are stuck tight to rocks, trying not to dry out. When the tide comes back in, they travel around eating algae, returning to their precise starting places before the water retreats once more.

At up to 20 centimetres in length, the Pacific banana slug is one of the world's largest slugs. While it looks like a lovely ripe 'nana, it tastes the way you might expect a slug to taste, and its slime numbs your tongue.

Gastropods are considered a delicacy in many countries. The French eat small land snails roasted in garlic and butter, while cooked winkles and whelks are commonly served as 'seafood'.

🔍 SIGNS OF LIFE:

☐ THE SEA

☐ THE LAND

☐ GARDENS

☐ FRENCH RESTAURANTS

oyster

mussels

Bivalves
🌐 About 9,000 species

Bivalves are aquatic headless molluscs with hinged shells that feed by filtering food from water. They include oysters, mussels, cockles, clams and scallops, and have long been an important food for humans.

cockle

scallop

The tropical giant clam lives in reefs and can be over a metre across. Despite lurid legends about attacking divers, it feeds on microscopic particles.

giant clam

Bivalves such as mussels and oysters can produce lustrous pearls if an irritant, like a grain of sand, gets inside. The grain is coated in layers of a protective mineral called nacre, building up over time. The world's largest pearl (65 centimetres wide) came from a giant clam and is valued at $100 million (over £77 million).

giant pearl

$100,000,000

🔍 SIGNS OF LIFE:

☐ THE SEA

☐ SEAFOOD COUNTERS

☐ HIGH-SECURITY BANK VAULTS

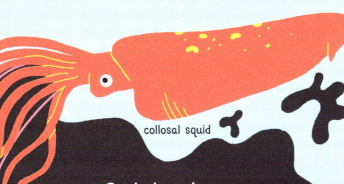
collosal squid

Cephalopods
🌐 Over 800 species

Cephalopod means 'head–foot'. These marine molluscs include octopuses, squid, cuttlefish and nautiloids. All have arms or tentacles, big brains, a parrot-like beak for crunching prey and the most advanced eyes of any invertebrate. They can also change colour, squirt ink to deceive predators and zoom away using jet propulsion!

At up to 14 metres long, the colossal squid is the world's largest living invertebrate. It also has the largest eye in the animal kingdom at 27 centimetres in diameter.

Despite being so big, the squid has never been caught alive and feeds on fish, which it grinds up to pass down a throat just 1 centimetre wide. Oh, and it has three hearts and blue blood too.

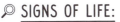
🔍 SIGNS OF LIFE:

☐ SEAFOOD RESTAURANTS

☐ THE SEA

☐ THE DEEP DARK OCEAN

Echinoderms
🌐 Over 7,000 species

Echinoderm means 'spiny skin'. This exclusively sea-dwelling group includes starfish, sea urchins and less well-known organisms such as brittle stars, sand dollars, sea cucumbers and sea lilies.

sea lily

sea cucumber

sea urchins

sand dollar

starfish

Gimme five!

Many echinoderms have five-point radial symmetry, seen in the classic starfish shape. However, the largest known starfish – the sunflower sea star – is 1 metre wide with 24 arms. Starfish have incredible powers of regeneration, being able to regrow missing limbs. In fact, some species can regrow a whole new starfish from a single arm!

sunflower sea star

🔍 SIGNS OF LIFE:

☐ THE SEA

☐ THE SHORE

Arthropods: Shake a Leg

Arthropod means 'jointed foot'. The members of this group have pairs of jointed limbs, a hard outer skeleton ('exoskeleton') and segmented bodies. Sea-dwelling trilobites were an early member, over 500 million years ago. Today the group is split into five main gangs: horseshoe crabs, arachnids, myriapods, crustaceans and insects (see page 42).

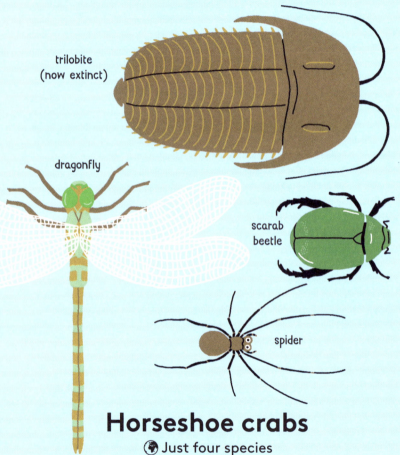

trilobite (now extinct)

dragonfly

scarab beetle

spider

Horseshoe crabs
🌐 Just four species

These are not actually crabs but 'living fossils' largely unchanged since they evolved 450 million years ago. The shape of their shells gives rise to their common name. Horseshoe crab eggs are an important food for fish, turtles and seabirds. Luckily, females lay up to 60,000 eggs at a time.

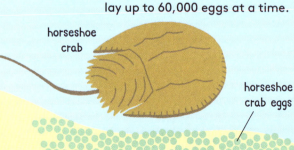

horseshoe crab

horseshoe crab eggs

Arachnids
🌐 Over 100,000 species

This arthropod group includes ticks, mites, scorpions and – most famously – spiders. Most arachnids have eight legs, a body in two parts and no wings, and almost all live on land or as parasites. Although spiders and scorpions can look scary, it is actually only tiny mites and ticks that might feed on us.

mite   tick   spider

The Mexican redknee tarantula is a popular pet, and rarely bites!

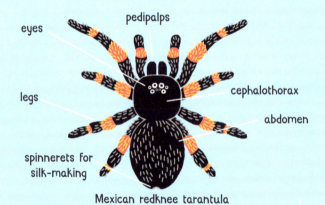

eyes
pedipalps
legs
cephalothorax
abdomen
spinnerets for silk-making

Mexican redknee tarantula

Spider v. bee

Fear of spiders is called arachnophobia, but they only ever bite in defence and most can't pierce our skin with their fangs. The funnel web spider of Australia is one of the world's most venomous spiders, yet a recent survey showed no deaths from spider bites in the country, compared to 25 deaths from bee stings.

funnel web spider

Put your foot in it?

Most scorpions have a front pair of pincers and a venomous stinger at the tip of a curving tail. Found in warm countries, they hunt other animals at night – seizing prey with their pincers and stinging to paralyse it.

Of over 1,000 species, only about 25 are harmful to humans, and that is mostly by accident – such as when someone puts on a shoe with a scorpion inside. Check first!

The deathstalker scorpion is one of the deadliest, and often illegal to keep as a pet.

SIGNS OF LIFE

☐ ALMOST ENTIR ON LAND

☐ CHECK YOUR SHOES!

Myriapods

🌐 About 16,000 species

Myriapod means 'thousand-footed', and this group includes millipedes and centipedes. Millipedes have an arched cross-section and eat decaying vegetation. Centipedes are flattened and carnivorous, often moving with surprising speed to grab prey and inject it with venom.

False legs

All centipedes have an odd number of pairs of legs, meaning none of them can have exactly 100 legs in total. 98 or 102 is the closest you can get.

The Peruvian giant yellow-leg centipede is the world's largest, at up to 30 centimetres long. It feeds on anything it can catch, including bats, and its bite can even kill humans.

Living leg-end

No living millipede actually has one thousand legs. A US species, *Illacme plenipes*, comes closest, with up to 750 legs – giving it the record for the most-legged animal, despite being only about 3 centimetres long!

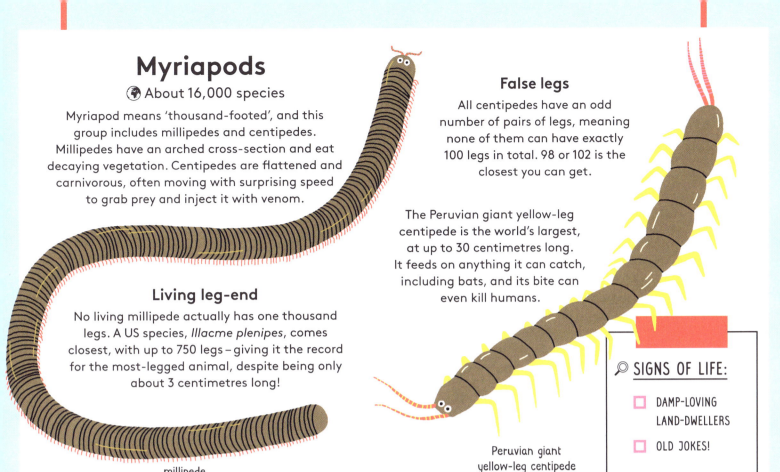

millipede

Peruvian giant yellow-leg centipede

🔎 SIGNS OF LIFE:

☐ DAMP-LOVING LAND-DWELLERS

☐ OLD JOKES!

Crustaceans

🌐 Over 67,000 species

Most crustaceans are aquatic animals with hard chalky shells, such as crabs, shrimps, prawns, crayfish and lobsters. The humble woodlouse lives on land, but even it prefers damp places. Zillions of paperclip-sized crustaceans called krill inhabit the world's oceans and are a vital food for everything from jellyfish to whales. Humans harvest and eat krill too, as well as enjoying larger species of crustacean as seafood.

The Japanese spider crab is the world's largest arthropod, with a leg-span of 5.5 metres!

prawn

crab

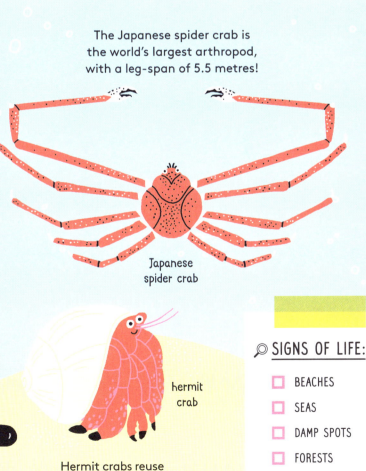

Japanese spider crab

The lobsters some people eat are actually blue in the wild. A pigment in their shells changes colour when they are cooked, turning them 'lobster pink'.

hermit crab

lobster

Hermit crabs reuse abandoned mollusc shells as their homes, trading up to a larger size as they grow!

🔎 SIGNS OF LIFE:

☐ BEACHES

☐ SEAS

☐ DAMP SPOTS

☐ FORESTS

☐ FISHMONGERS

Insects: Six Legs Good

🌐 About 65,000 species

Insects have six legs and a body in three parts: head, thorax, abdomen. All but a few lay eggs, and many have wings. Insects were, in fact, the first flying organisms, about 406 million years ago.

Today, insects show a range of size, shape, form, food, lifecycle, habitat and behaviour, and many change in appearance as they grow, a process known as 'metamorphosis'. A butterfly, for example, hatches from an egg into a hungry caterpillar. It then eats and grows, eventually forming a 'chrysalis' (or 'pupa'), before emerging as an adult.

egg   caterpillar   pupa   butterfly

Insects are so amazingly abundant that they account for nine out of every ten animals on the planet. Here is what that fact looks like:

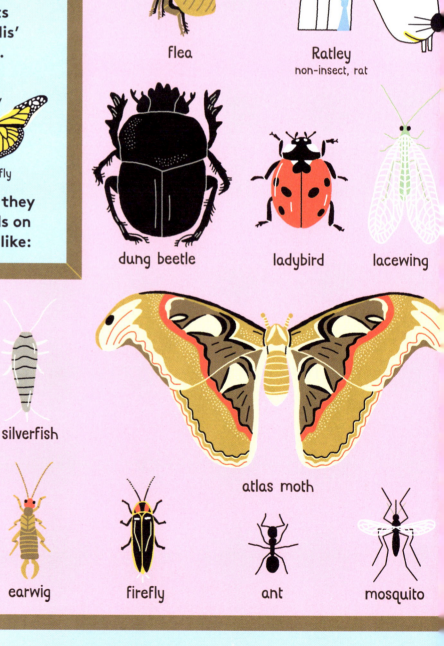

louse

cockroach

flea

Ratley
non-insect, rat

dung beetle   ladybird   lacewing

atlas moth

stick insect   cricket   silverfish   earwig   firefly   ant   mosquito

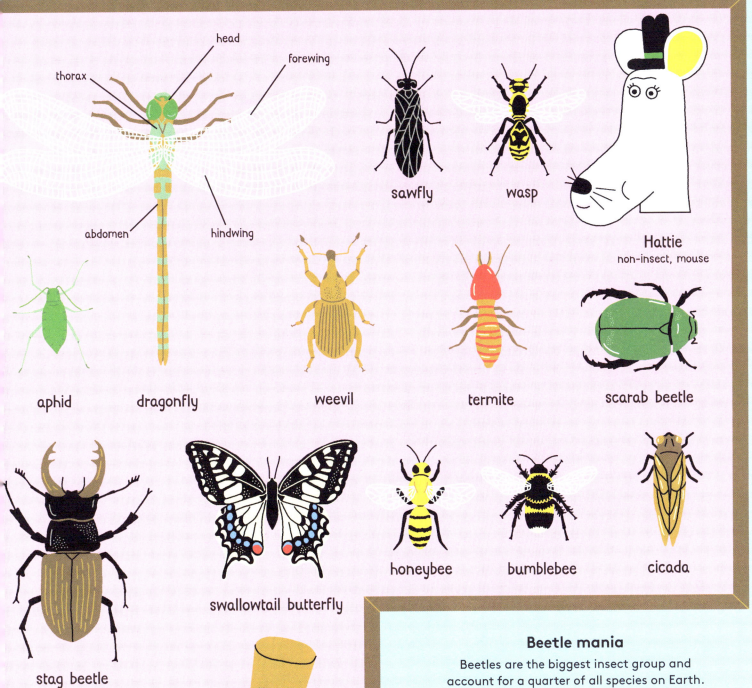

thorax

head

forewing

abdomen

hindwing

dragonfly

sawfly

wasp

Hattie
non-insect, mouse

aphid

weevil

termite

scarab beetle

stag beetle

swallowtail butterfly

honeybee

bumblebee

cicada

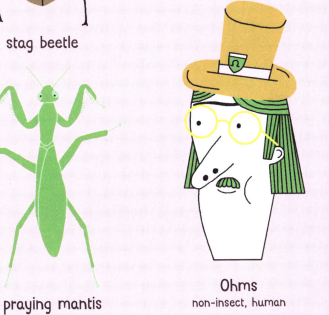

praying mantis

Ohms
non-insect, human

Beetle mania

Beetles are the biggest insect group and account for a quarter of all species on Earth. No wonder Charles Darwin (see pages 44–45) was mad about them!

🔍 SIGNS OF LIFE:

☐ EVERYWHERE EXCEPT THE OCEANS

LIFE STORIES

IN NOVEMBER 1859, A BIOLOGY BOOK BECAME A BESTSELLER...

ON THE ORIGIN OF SPECIES

FIRST EDITION

CHARLES DARWIN

...DESPITE CONTAINING ONLY ONE (DULL) ILLUSTRATION!

ITS AUTHOR, BIO-BOFFIN CHARLES DARWIN*, HAD BEEN WORKING ON IT SECRETLY FOR THE PAST TWENTY YEARS...

You could say it 'evolved' slowly...

*UK, 1809–1882

THE BOOK OUTLINED HIS THEORY ON HOW ORGANISMS CHANGED OVER TIME TO PRODUCE NEW SPECIES...

Fancy a change?

Yes – in theory...

WE CALL THE PROCESS 'EVOLUTION', BUT THEN IT WAS KNOWN AS 'TRANSMUTATION'.

DARWIN'S BOOK WAS CONSIDERED DANGEROUS, AS IT OPPOSED THE IDEA OF DIVINE CREATION AND SUGGESTED HUMANS WERE PART OF NATURE...

My critics went wild!

BUT HOW DID IT COME ABOUT? WELL...

...LIKE LINNAEUS (SEE PAGES 30–31), DARWIN WAS DESTINED TO BE A DOCTOR BUT FOUND IT ALL TOO GORY.

MMWWWHHH!*

*TRANSLATION: 'I'M NOT CUT OUT FOR SURGERY!'

HIS REAL PASSION WAS FOR NATURAL HISTORY – ESPECIALLY COLLECTING BEETLES...

BWAABBBH!*

*TRANSLATION: 'I HAVE A RARE BEETLE IN MY MOUTH!' (HE DID ACTUALLY DO THIS!)

AGED 22, HE JOINED A LONG VOYAGE AS THE SHIP'S NATURALIST ON BOARD HMS *BEAGLE* – A BRITISH NAVY VESSEL MAPPING THE COASTS OF MANY COUNTRIES...

PLYMOUTH (UK)

GALAPAGOS ISLANDS

BLURRRK!*

DEPARTED PLYMOUTH, UK, 1831. DOCKED FALMOUTH, UK, 1836.
*TRANSLATION: 'I GOT VERY SEASICK!'

EACH TIME THE *BEAGLE* LANDED, DARWIN COLLECTED SPECIMENS THAT HE SENT BACK FOR EXPERTS TO EXAMINE...

Can you guess what they are?... Well, were...

PENGUIN

?

FOSSIL BONE

ARMADILLO

THEY CAN STILL BE SEEN IN MUSEUMS.

IN SOUTH AMERICA, SOME GIANT FOSSILS SET HIM THINKING...

This skull is from an extinct giant sloth, yet smaller, similar-looking sloths are alive today... Hmm...

IN AUTUMN 1835, THE *BEAGLE* VISITED THE REMOTE GALAPAGOS ISLANDS, ALMOST 1,000 KILOMETRES FROM ECUADOR...

GALAPAGOS ISLANDS

EACH ISLAND HAD ANIMALS FOUND NOWHERE ELSE – INCLUDING SMALL BIRDS WITH WIDELY VARYING BEAKS...

 THICK BEAK – CRACKS SEEDS

 THIN BEAK – EATS INSECTS

 USES TOOLS TO FIND INSECTS

 DRINKS BLOOD FROM SEABIRDS

THERE WERE ABOUT 15 DIFFERENT SPECIES, WHICH HE TOOK HOME FOR A TOP BIRD BOD TO EXAMINE...

THE BIRD BOD HAD SOME EXCITING NEWS!

They differ widely but they are all finches!

Hmm...

KNOWN AS 'DARWIN'S FINCHES', THEY SET HIM THINKING FOR SEVERAL YEARS...

DARWIN FIGURED THEY HAD A COMMON ANCESTOR THAT HAD LANDED ON THE ISLANDS AGES AGO. FOOD WAS LIMITED AND, OVER TIME, DESCENDANTS OF THOSE FIRST BIRDS HAD TURNED TO EATING DIFFERENT THINGS, DEVELOPING BEAKS MOST SUITED TO THEIR FOODS. LESS SUCCESSFUL BIRDS ATE LESS, BRED LESS AND, IN THE END, DIED OUT.

I called this 'natural selection'.

Older Darwin

ALSO KNOWN AS 'SURVIVAL OF THE FITTEST'.

AS THE DIFFERENCES BETWEEN BIRDS INCREASED, NEW SPECIES WERE CREATED, THOUGH THEY STILL SHARED A COMMON ANCESTOR. THIS IS WHAT DARWIN HAD SEEN IN THE FOSSIL RECORD...

ALL LIFE TODAY has evolved and shares ancestors with fossils found in rocks!

DARWIN KNEW HIS IDEAS WOULD ANGER RELIGIOUS PEOPLE, SO HE WORKED ON THEM IN SECRET UNTIL, IN 1858, HE HEARD FROM ANOTHER NATURALIST, ALFRED RUSSEL WALLACE (1823–1913)...

I had hit on the same idea!

Dear Mr Darwin

TODAY, DARWIN AND WALLACE SHARE THE CREDIT FOR THE THEORY.

DARWIN HURRIED TO GET INTO PRINT FIRST... BUT NOT EVERYONE ACCEPTED HIS IDEAS...

ON THE ORIGIN OF SPECIES CHARLES DARWIN

He's making monkeys of us all!

OVER 150 YEARS LATER, MOST SCIENTISTS CONSIDER EVOLUTION TO BE A FACT.

IN A LATER BOOK*, DARWIN ARGUED DIRECTLY THAT HUMANS AND APES HAD COMMON ANCESTORS. SOME STILL FELT THIS WAS A BAREFACED LIE...

But by then I had a big white beard!

THE DESCENT OF MAN CHARLES DARWIN

*THE DESCENT OF MAN, 1871.

THE THEORY OF EVOLUTION LIVES ON, BUT 'DANGEROUS' DARWIN DIED IN 1882. SURPRISINGLY, PERHAPS, HE WAS BURIED IN WESTMINSTER ABBEY, LONDON – A FAMOUS RELIGIOUS BUILDING!

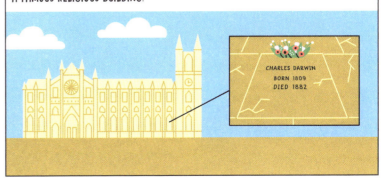

CHARLES DARWIN BORN 1809 DIED 1882

Fish: Making a Splash

No bones about it, all the animals examined so far have been so-called invertebrates. If they have any sort of hard skeleton, it is on the outside of their bodies, as seen in sea urchins, crabs, insects and others.

Our search for the signs of life now takes in all those animals with no visible means of support: vertebrates, or animals with a stiff jointed skeleton hidden inside them. Technically, scientists prefer to call them 'chordates' (see the box opposite) – a group that includes Hattie, Ratley and humans. Let's begin by examining our aquatic cousins, fish.

Fish

Fish are fin-tastic! You can find them in high mountain streams, the deepest oceans and even in lightless underground lakes where eyes are pointless and have disappeared. All fish live in water and use gills to extract the dissolved oxygen they need to breathe. Most also have fins for swimming and bodies covered in scales.

An important food for some humans, fish fall into three groups: jawless fish; those with skeletons made of cartilage (such as sharks and rays); and bony fish (such as cod and salmon).

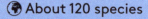

Jawless fish

🌐 About 120 species

The first fish appeared about 530 million years ago and had no jaws. Their modern relatives are lampreys – a parasitic eel-shaped fish that sticks to prey using a sucker-like mouth – and the hagfish, a mud-dwelling scavenger that knots itself around rotting flesh to break it up. It also oozes slime!

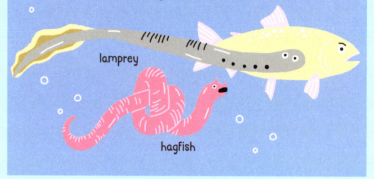

lamprey

hagfish

Cartilaginous fish

🌐 Over 700 species

Cartilage is the flexible material you can feel between your nostrils when you put a finger up your nose. It forms the skeletons of sharks, skates, rays and ratfish – named for their rat-like tails. Mostly marine, all cartilaginous fish have teeth that are continually replaced throughout their lives, some of which are rather scary-looking!

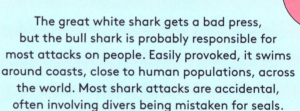

great white shark

The great white shark gets a bad press, but the bull shark is probably responsible for most attacks on people. Easily provoked, it swims around coasts, close to human populations, across the world. Most shark attacks are accidental, often involving divers being mistaken for seals.

Sharks actually play a vital role in the sea, cleaning up dead and dying animals, and we should think of them as friends!

At over 18 metres long, the whale shark is the largest living fish. Despite its size, it only eats tiny plankton, filter-feeding by swimming along with its mouth open wide. How rude!

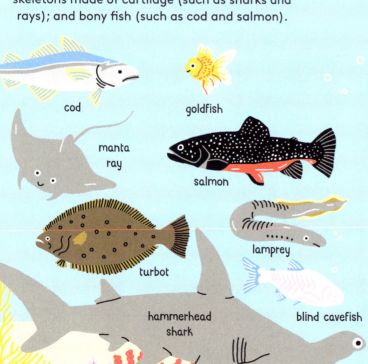

cod

goldfish

manta ray

salmon

turbot

lamprey

hammerhead shark

blind cavefish

whale shark

Bony fish

🌐 Over 28,000 species

Unlike sharks, these have bony skeletons and an air-filled sac in their bodies, called a 'swim-bladder', which helps them float.

Bony fish have an amazing range of shapes and include eels, anchovies, herrings, catfish, salmon, seahorses, tuna, groupers, marlin, mackerel and all the oddities of the dark, deep seas. Some members of this group have flat, fan-shaped fins called 'ray-fins', others have fleshy, muscular lobe-fins (thought to have evolved into the first limbs 400 million years ago).

coelacanth

The coelacanth is a 'living fossil'. It was thought to have become extinct 66 million years ago, but a specimen was caught off South Africa in 1938, surprising the world. Little is known about them, but they have been seen happily swimming upside down!

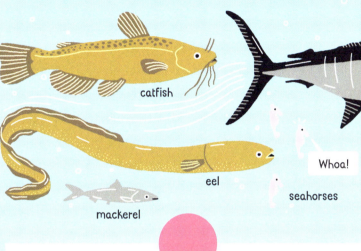

catfish

eel

mackerel

Whoa!

seahorses

The streamlined black marlin is the world's fastest fish at 130 kilometres per hour. The slowest fish is the dwarf seahorse, which takes an hour to swim little more than a metre.

black marlin

Pufferfish swallow water to frighten off predators, swelling up instantly. Their stomachs also contain a deadly toxin that can be fatal to humans. However, they are eaten as a delicacy in Japan, cooked by chefs specially trained to make them safe.

pufferfish

Strike a chord

The embryos of all vertebrates, including humans, develop a small flexible rod called a notochord as they grow. This tiny rod disappears before birth.

Animals with a notochord are called 'chordates', but the group also includes some odd little invertebrates.

notochord

Lancelets are small – up to 5 centimetres long – and almost transparent. They feed by filtering particles from the warm waters in which they live.

lancelet

Sea squirts are bag-like animals that also filter-feed. Often colourful and strangely beautiful, they suck water in through one hole and expel it from another, hence their common name.

sea squirt

The deep sea-dwelling blobfish has been called the world's ugliest animal, but hauling it to the surface actually changes its appearance.

BEFORE   blobfish   AFTER

🔍 SIGNS OF LIFE:

☐ KITCHEN CUPBOARDS

☐ FREEZER

☐ FISHMONGER

☐ ZOO

☐ AQUARIUM

☐ SEASIDE

☐ FISH AND CHIP SHOP

mudskipper

The mudskipper is literally a fish out of water. Found in tropical swamps, it can crawl out of the water and breathe on land through its wet skin and air trapped in its gills. Up to 30 centimetres long, mudskippers are a good clue to how life left the ocean for the land.

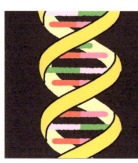

LIFE STORIES

THERE WAS A HITCH WITH DARWIN'S THEORY OF EVOLUTION (SEE PAGE 44-45) - NO ONE KNEW HOW OFFSPRING INHERITED TRAITS FROM THEIR PARENTS...

A trait is a characteristic, like eye colour or, er, baldness... COUGH!

SO HOW DID A NUT-EATING GROUND FINCH WITH A BIGGER AND BETTER BEAK PASS THIS TRAIT ON TO ITS YOUNG?

Like father, like son...

Don't speak with your beak full!

GOOD QUESTION!

FARMERS HAD LONG CROSS-BRED PLANTS AND ANIMALS TO PRODUCE NEW VARIETIES, AND DARWIN DID THE SAME WITH PIGEONS, CREATING BIRDS WITH DIFFERENT TRAITS...

This is called artificial selection.

Coo!

DESPITE BEING DEAD CLEVER, DARWIN DIDN'T KNOW HOW TRAITS WERE PASSED ON. INSTEAD, AN AUGUSTINIAN MONK* WAS QUIETLY CARRYING OUT SOME EXPERIMENTS...

I breed peas, hybrid peas!

common pea (Pisum sativum L.)

*GREGOR MENDEL, CZECH REPUBLIC, 1822-1884

MENDEL LOOKED AT TRAITS IN PEA PLANTS, IN WHICH THE SEEDS OF ANY SINGLE PLANT ARE EITHER ALL GREEN OR ALL YELLOW. MENDEL CROSS-BRED GREEN- AND YELLOW-SEEDED PLANTS TO SEE WHAT RESULTED...

I got all yellow seeds!

NEVER A BLEND OF THE TWO COLOURS.

HE THEN GREW THESE YELLOW SEEDS AND CROSS-BRED ALL THE PLANTS. THIS TIME HE GOT A SURPRISE...

Green-seeded plants reappeared!

IN A RATIO OF 3 YELLOW TO 1 GREEN.

MENDEL REALISED THAT ONE 'FACTOR' FOR A TRAIT CAME FROM EACH PARENT, AND THAT SOME FACTORS WERE DOMINANT OVER OTHERS...

Some simple maths showed me how!

Y	Y
Y	YY	Yy
Y	yY	yy

IN WILD PEAS, THE 'YELLOW' FACTOR IS DOMINANT. BUT WE GROW GREEN PEAS BECAUSE PEOPLE PREFER THE COLOUR!

TODAY, MENDEL IS KNOWN AS THE 'FATHER OF GENETICS' - THE STUDY OF INHERITED CHARACTERISTICS - BUT HIS WORK WAS IGNORED FOR DECADES...

Oh well, I still liked peas! Yum!

IT TOOK UNTIL 1910 TO SHOW THAT MENDEL'S 'FACTORS' WERE TINY CODED CHEMICAL INSTRUCTIONS CALLED 'GENES', LOCATED ON THE CHROMOSOMES IN THE NUCLEI OF CELLS.

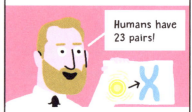

Humans have 23 pairs!

THOMAS HUNT MORGAN, USA, 1866-1945

IT THEN TOOK DECADES TO SHOW THAT CHROMOSOMES WERE MOLECULES OF A CHEMICAL CALLED DNA (DEOXYRIBONUCLEIC ACID), AND A LITTLE LONGER TO REVEAL ITS STRUCTURE. FRANCIS CRICK AND JAMES WATSON DID THIS IN 1953 WITH THE HELP OF ROSALIND FRANKLIN.

We three did that!

GENES ARE SHORT SECTIONS ON A DNA MOLECULE THAT ARE CODE FOR A TRAIT. YOU INHERIT THEM FROM YOUR PARENTS AND SOMETIMES THEY CHANGE ('MUTATE') TO PRODUCE A NEW TRAIT - ONE THAT MIGHT OR MIGHT NOT BE USEFUL...

Dad, this beak is bonkers!

Could come in handy one day, son...

HUMANS, RATS AND MICE ALL HAVE ABOUT 25,000 GENES. SCIENTISTS NOW SAY THAT EVERY LIVING THING - INCLUDING YOU - HAS 355 GENES IN COMMON WITH LUCA (THE LAST UNIVERSAL COMMON ANCESTOR), WHICH LIVED ON EARTH ABOUT 4 BILLION YEARS AGO...

I'm LUCA, how's life treating you?

ISN'T THAT AMAZING?!

Amphibians: Water Babies

🌐 Over 8,000 species

Amphibians are chordates. The name 'amphibian' means 'both kinds of life': land and water. Amphibians include frogs, toads, newts, salamanders and some odd limbless members called caecilians ('SEE-SILLY-ANS').

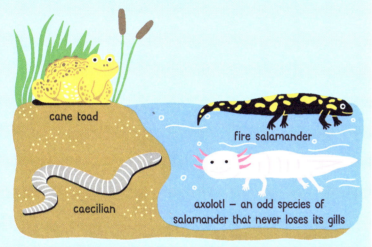

cane toad

fire salamander

caecilian

axolotl – an odd species of salamander that never loses its gills

All need water in their lifecycles. For example, frogs lay their eggs (spawn) in ponds. These hatch into tadpoles and live aquatically – breathing with gills – before changing into their final form. Young frogs then leave the water, coming back later to breed.

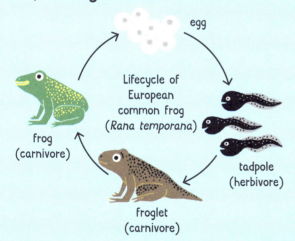

egg

Lifecycle of European common frog (*Rana temporana*)

frog (carnivore)

tadpole (herbivore)

froglet (carnivore)

300 million years ago, giant amphibians such as *Eryops* ruled the land.

Eryops was up to 3 metres long

Frogs and toads

90% of amphibians are frogs. Frogs tend to have smooth skins and hop, while toads have warty skins and crawl. Amphibians breathe through their skins and so must keep them wet. And you won't get warts from touching a toad!

frog

toad

The African goliath frog is the world's largest, at over 30 centimetres long. The smallest, however, lives in forests in Papua New Guinea and is just over 7 millimetres long. Here it is, actual size:

South American poison dart frogs have highly toxic chemicals in their skin that serve to deter predators. Many are brightly coloured as a warning not to eat them. Native people extract the poisons to place on darts used in hunting. Most are only a few centimetres in size.

South American poison dart frogs

Frogs can't swallow without closing their eyes. The bulge of their eyeballs inside their mouths helps to force food down their throats.

Salamanders and newts

These both look a little like lizards, with their long tails. In the breeding season, male great crested newts develop orange bellies and wonderful jagged crests that they hope will impress females enough to mate with them.

male great crested newt

female great crested newt

Don't let them croak!

Half the world's amphibians are at risk of extinction from hunting, habitat loss, disease and pollution. Help them out by putting in a pond!

🔍 SIGNS OF LIFE:

☐ LAKES

☐ PONDS

☐ RIVERS

☐ ZOOS

Reptiles: Wizard Lizards and Great Snakes

🌐 Over 10,000 species

Reptiles rock! Today, reptiles can be found on every continent except Antarctica, where it is just too cold. Most have dry, scaly skins and lay hard-shelled eggs, freeing them from needing water to breed.

lizard

tortoise

python

turtle

Tyrannosaurus rex

Dimetrodon

alligator

gharial

The group includes crocodiles, caimans, alligators, gharials, snakes, lizards, worm-lizards, turtles, tortoises, and terrapins. And – if the films were true – it might once again include live dinosaurs!

Snakes

🌐 3,600 species

Snakes are not slimy, though they certainly do slither. Most have dry scales made of a material similar to fingernails. In order to grow, many have to shed their skins, beginning from the head and leaving behind a ghostly hollow copy.

The skull bones of snakes are joined in a way that allows them to swallow prey many times bigger than themselves. The egg-eating snake forces down whole eggs, helped by the fact that it doesn't have teeth!

Some snakes, such as boa constrictors, squeeze their prey to death, eventually stopping it from breathing. Many snakes have curved fangs for capturing prey, but only 10% of snakes inject venom to paralyse their victims. At over 5 metres long, the king cobra is the world's longest venomous snake, and its bite is so deadly it can kill an elephant, never mind a human!

boa constrictor

king cobra

Unless you're a frog, the European grass snake is harmless. If scared by a human or a predator, it can play dead, lying on its back with its tongue out. It also produces a foul-smelling liquid.

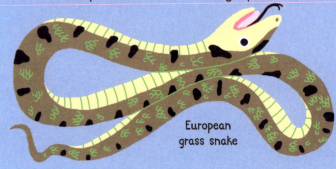

European grass snake

Turtles and tortoises

🌍 About 350 species

These organisms have hardly changed for 200 million years, yet today many are highly endangered. In some countries they are all called turtles, though to most the word 'turtle' means species that live in water, and 'tortoise' means their slow-moving, land-living relatives.

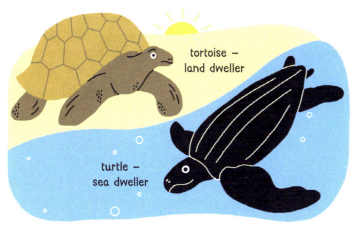

tortoise – land dweller

turtle – sea dweller

The Galapagos giant tortoise is the slowest known reptile, with a speed on land of just 0.3 kilometres per hour. However, as it eats plants, it doesn't need to hurry!

The leatherback sea turtle is the largest alive – the length of a human, with a giant leathery shell. It swims vast distances across oceans, hunting for jellyfish, and is the fastest-moving reptile, with a top speed of over 35 kilometres per hour.

Crocodiles and alligators

🌍 Just 22 species

All crocodilians like warm tropical conditions and live around water. They eat meat, and the largest of them – the saltwater crocodile of Asia and Australia – is known to attack humans for food. Males grow up to 6 metres long and hunt by drowning their prey or swallowing it whole. Super-fierce, they have even been seen to hunt sharks!

Many crocodilians are hunted for food or for their skins, which are made into shoes and handbags. In some countries, crocodiles are farmed, but luckily the trade in many wild reptile products is now widely banned, though it still goes on illegally.

NO SWIMMING!

crocodile

Lizards

🌍 About 4,600 species

Most lizards have four legs and a tail, though some – such as so-called slow-worms – are legless.

Eek!

chameleon

Chameleons catch insects by catapulting their sticky-ended tongues, which are often longer than their bodies. They can swivel their eyes to look forwards and backwards at the same time. Famously, they can also change colour – though this is not to camouflage themselves. Instead, it shows what mood they are in!

In hot countries, many humans share their homes with helpful insect-catching lizards.

Thanks to microscopic hairs on their feet, geckos have an amazing ability to scuttle over walls and ceilings.

The basilisk lizard of Central American rainforests can actually run on water!

gecko

basilisk lizard

The Indonesian Komodo dragon is the largest living lizard. It is over 3 metres long, with toxic saliva, and a single bite can kill a water buffalo. Compare it with the world's smallest chameleon, which comes from Madagascar and is less than the size of a fingernail!

15 MILLIMETRES

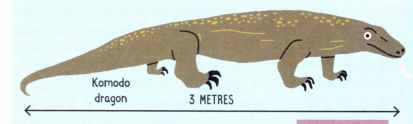

Komodo dragon

3 METRES

Worm lizards

🌍 About 200 species

These strange creatures are neither snakes nor true lizards, though they look a bit like both. Almost blind, they burrow into the ground in Africa and the Americas in search of prey.

🔍 SIGNS OF LIFE:

☐ OCEANS

☐ JUNGLES

☐ NICE WARM HOMES

worm lizard

Birds: Winging it

🌐 About 10,000 species, possibly many more

Detecting birds is one of the most popular pastimes in the world. Birdwatchers flock to catch a glimpse of rare specimens of these feathery descendants of dinosaurs. As Aristotle (see page 13) recognised over 2,000 years ago, birds have a beak, feathers, warm blood, hard-shelled eggs and wings, though not all of them can fly.

In the 150 million years since they first appeared, birds have evolved many amazing solutions for surviving almost everywhere on Earth, reflected in their shape, size, colour, calls, behaviour and diet. As Charles Darwin (see pages 44–45) noted with his Galapagos finches, beaks speak volumes. So, here are some avian heads and tales.

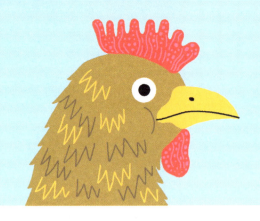

Chicken

The domestic chicken is the most abundant bird on the planet, with over 22 billion at any one time. The combined weight of chickens alone is greater than that of all wild birds.

Archaeopteryx fossil

In 1861, what is probably the world's most important fossil was found in Germany (see page 37). *Archaeopteryx* had a tail and teeth, like a reptile, and a beak and feathers, like a bird.

Halfway between both groups, it is powerful evidence for evolution.

African ostrich

The African ostrich is the world's largest bird, at over 2 metres tall. Flightless, it can run up to 70 kilometres per hour – another avian record – and lays the largest egg of any living animal.

Cooked, a single ostrich egg is the equivalent of two dozen hen's eggs. Ostriches also have the largest eyes of any land animal.

New Zealand kiwi

Most birds rely on sight rather than smell. The nocturnal New Zealand kiwi has nostrils at the tip of its long beak with which it sniffs out earthworms in the dark. It can also sense them moving.

Emperor penguin

Emperor penguins live on Antarctic ice. The female lays a single egg, which she leaves for the male to incubate while she spends the winter hunting for fish. The male doesn't eat until she returns in the spring, just as the egg hatches. Flightless, penguins have wings that work as flippers, and they swim brilliantly.

Bee hummingbird

The bee hummingbird of Cuba is the world's smallest bird and has the smallest egg. Just 6 centimetres long, an adult weighs less than three paperclips. It feeds on nectar, beats its wings up to 200 times a second and can fly backwards!

Australian pelican

The Australian pelican has the biggest beak, or bill, the longest on record being 50 centimetres. They eat mainly fish, but there are stories of pelicans in parks wolfing down pigeons and even small dogs.

Eggs

Birds' eggs vary widely. Species that fly actively for long periods, such as swallows, lay pointy, streamlined eggs. Owls, by contrast, fly less and lay spherical eggs.

swallow eggs

owl egg

Cuckoos lay their eggs in the nests of other birds, leaving a different species to raise them. Amazingly, they produce eggs that look just like the eggs of their host bird.

Vanishing trick

Eggshells are mostly calcium carbonate (chalk). They have tiny pores to allow the embryo inside to breathe, and are very strong for their weight. As an eggs-periment, place a raw hen's egg in vinegar for a few days and you can dissolve the shell to reveal the membrane that would surround the developing chick.

Sulphur-crested cockatoo

Snowball, a sulphur-crested cockatoo, became an Internet sensation after being filmed dancing to music. Scientists thought only humans danced spontaneously, but Snowball has at least 14 different moves – including head-banging – and likes the music of Queen and Cyndi Lauper.

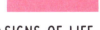

SIGNS OF LIFE:

- ☐ THE FRIDGE
- ☐ PILLOWS
- ☐ DUVETS
- ☐ EVERYWHERE – GRAB SOME BINOCULARS!

Birds of prey

Birds of prey such as owls and hawks have hooked beaks for tearing flesh and forward-facing eyes for spotting victims. Peregrine falcons can dive at over 300 kilometres per hour, making them the fastest (non-human) animals on the planet!

Mammals: The Fur Brigade

🌐 Over 5,400 species

Eat a sandwich, drink a glass of milk, ruffle your hair: you have just experienced three things unique to mammals. Only mammals have a single-piece lower jaw and a mix of teeth that allow them to chew, rather than just bite, rip or peck. They are the only animals that produce milk to feed their young. Only mammals have hair or fur on their bodies.

Humans are mammals, of course – the most successful and intelligent members of a small but massively diverse group of animals that have taken furry, warm-blooded, milky life into every corner of the planet.

We could be accused of being biased here, but mammals are marvellous. Take a look at the evidence!

The white stuff

Carl Linnaeus (see pages 30–31), a mammal, invented the term 'mammal' in 1758. It refers to the mammary glands or teats from which nursing females secrete milk to feed their offspring. Humans are the only mammals to continue drinking milk as adults, though this milk comes from cows, sheep and goats.

Great Expectations

Most – but not all – mammals grow their offspring inside their bodies, attached to a special organ called a placenta. This feeds the baby and takes away its waste. Mammals then give birth to live young. Known as 'gestation', pregnancy for humans takes about 9 months. For elephants, it is over 20 months – the longest for any mammal.

A small number of primitive mammals called monotremes lay eggs, which is a clue to their reptilian ancestry. These include the odd-looking echidna and duck-billed platypus, both found in Australia. Lacking teats or nipples, mothers simply express milk on to their fur for babies to lap up.

A third way of raising offspring is inside a pouch. This group – known as 'marsupials' – includes wallabies, wombats, possums, koalas and kangaroos. A kangaroo's pouch contains the teats, and the newly born tiny, blind, hairless little joey climbs laboriously up its mother's tummy to get inside. Despite this hard start in life, red kangaroos are a pest in many places, as well as being the largest living marsupials.

Fur enough

Fur protects mammals, aids in display, camouflage and courtship, and helps them keep a constant body temperature in both hot and cold habitats. Whales and dolphins are hairless, while the naked mole-rat of East Africa has just a few wispy bits. Porcupines have modified their hair to form prickly defensive spines. Sadly, many mammals have been hunted to extinction for their beautiful fur.

Smell and tell

Mammals secrete scents that carry complex signals about their age, status, gender, mood and readiness to mate. Tigers are very territorial. They spray trees with a mixture of pee and special secretions that tell other tigers to back off. Weirdly, tiger urine is said to smell like buttered popcorn.

Fur also helps to spread scents, which may be why adult humans have hairy armpits.

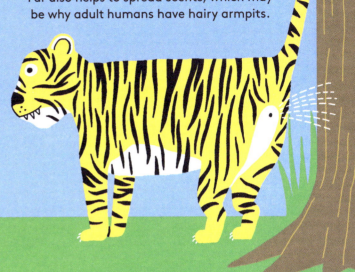

The eyes have it

Hunting mammals, such as lions and leopards, have forward-facing eyes to focus on prey, while prey species, such as antelopes and rabbits, have side-facing eyes to scan for threats.

However, the star-nosed mole of North America is totally blind, feeling for food with 22 pink fleshy 'feelers' around its nose. These are hyper-sensitive, allowing the mole to react so quickly that it has been declared the fastest-eating mammal in the world. Food disappears in a matter of milliseconds!

🔍 SIGNS OF LIFE:

☐ LOOK AROUND YOU

☐ LOOK IN A MIRROR!

The whole tooth

Mammals are the only animals with a lower jaw that allows chewing. They also have specialised teeth for different jobs: incisors for biting, canines for tearing and molars for grinding. In rodents, like Ratley and Hattie, the incisors keep growing all through life. Rodents must gnaw constantly to wear them down, otherwise the teeth can grow so long they pierce their skulls!

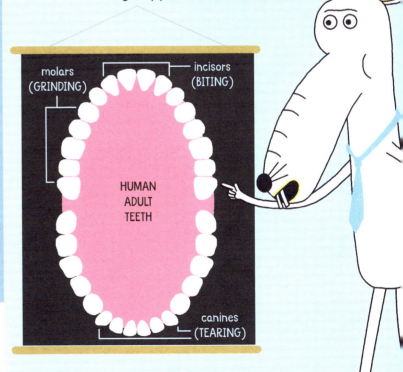

molars (GRINDING)

incisors (BITING)

HUMAN ADULT TEETH

canines (TEARING)

Mammal Groups: Feeding and Breeding

Humans, being human, can't quite agree how best to divide all their fellow mammals into groups. Most place them into about 26 different smaller groups known as 'orders'.

There are too many mammals to mention them all, so here are some of the most amazing!

Order: Edentata

This order includes anteaters, sloths and armadillos. They are found in the Americas and all lack front teeth.

Sloths are the world's slowest-moving mammals. Spending most of their time hanging upside down in trees in South American rainforests, they can manage to cover only about 5 metres an hour. They move so slowly that algae and insects grow in their fur, though, with strong arms and large claws, they are speedy swimmers.

Order: Diprotodontia

This order includes wallabies, possums, wombats, kangaroos and koalas – all of which keep their young in a pouch (see page 54).

Koalas aren't bears (though often wrongly referred to as such), they are cute-looking marsupials found in Australia, usually in the branches of eucalyptus trees. Eucalyptus leaves aren't very nutritious, so the koala sleeps for 20 hours a day to save energy. Its eucalyptus diet also means its poo smells like cough sweets!

Order: Artiodactyla

This order includes deer, camels, pigs, sheep, antelopes, goats, cattle, hippos and giraffes. They all have hooves that are divided ('cloven') into two toes.

Giraffes are the tallest living mammals. They can tower up to 6 metres and have to spread their front legs in order to get their heads low enough to drink. They rip leaves from tall trees with their blue tongues, and yet have no more bones in their necks than humans: just seven vertebrae.

Order: Carnivora

This order includes meat-eaters such as bears, weasels, badgers, seals, wolves, dogs and cats.

The cheetah lives in African forests and savannahs (grassy plains), where it chases down herbivores including gazelles and impala. Unlike lions and tigers, it hunts during the day rather than at night. In short bursts it can reach 112 kilometres per hour, making it the fastest living land mammal.

Order: Rodentia

Rodents are the largest order of mammals, with about 40% of all mammal species. It includes rats, mice, lemmings, hamsters, gerbils, squirrels and its largest member, the metre-long capybara of South America. They are united by all having pairs of continuously-growing upper and lower incisor teeth.

So-called flying squirrels glide between trees using a stretched membrane of skin like a wing. They can glide for up to 400 metres.

Order: Chiroptera

'Chiroptera' is Greek for 'hand-wings', bats being the only mammals that can truly fly, not just glide. Bats are the second largest order of mammals, after rodents. Some eat fruit and many eat insects, which they track using echolocation (sending out high-frequency sounds that bounce back to them from their prey).

Vampire bats have incredibly sharp teeth and feed on the blood of livestock in Central and South America, and on the odd sleeping human, too, if they leave a window open...

Order: Pholidota

This order contains the only living mammals wholly covered in scales. Known as pangolins, they look fierce, but these nocturnal African and Asian animals are only dangerous to ants and termites.

When alarmed, pangolins curl into a ball. They are, unfortunately, the world's most illegally trafficked animal. They are killed for their scales and meat.

Out of order

Some species of mammals are close enough to be cross-bred to produce odd hybrids. A wholphin is a cross between a killer whale and a dolphin. A lion and a tiger can give you either a liger or a tigon. Crossing a grizzly bear and a polar bear gives you a grolar or a pizzly – same animal, two names.

whale + dolphin = wholphin

polar bear + grizzly bear = grolar bear

tiger + lion = liger

Small beginnings

Scientists think the ancestor of all placental mammals, including humans, was a small shrew-sized insect-eater that was around at the time of the dinosaurs. Meet your 'many-many-million-times-over' great-grandparent!

Primates: Monkey Business

🌐 Several hundred species

Another order of mammals, primates – these are your homeys. This order includes lemurs, marmosets, tamarins, chimpanzees, orangutans, bonobos, gorillas, gibbons and baboons. Primates have large brains and gripping hands, often with opposable thumbs – vital for the many members that live in trees.

marmoset tamarin bonobo gibbon baboon

Great apes

Common chimpanzees in Africa have taught themselves to use tools. The famous primate scientist Jane Goodall observed chimps repeatedly poking twigs into termite nests. Angry termites clamped on to the twigs with their jaws and the chimps then ate them like insect lollipops!

Chimps and bonobos are our closest relatives, sharing 99% of our genes. Given this, scientists still aren't sure why we look and behave so differently.

Great gorillas

The eastern lowland gorilla of the African Congo is the largest living primate. At 1.85 metres, they stand no taller than humans but weigh three times as much. Despite their size and strength, they eat fruit and leaves and only attack humans if provoked.

The film *King Kong* was wrong!

Man alive!

Modern humans have been around for about 350,000 years. Our ancestors came from eastern Africa, and until about 40,000 years ago, we shared the planet with stockier and stronger Neanderthals. The species (humans and Neanderthals) interbred, and a small percentage of our DNA is actually Neanderthal.

🧪 Finger tip

Touch together the tips of your thumb and little finger. Most – but not all – people should see a short little tendon raised in their wrist. This serves no purpose today, but comes from the times when our ancestors swung in trees.

We also show other signs of much earlier ancestry:

- The coccyx at the base of your spine is the remnant of a lost tail.

- Newborn humans will grasp things tightly – a reflex that baby monkeys need to keep hold of their mothers.

- We all possess the same muscles that animals have for moving their ears in response to sounds. Some people can use them to wiggle their ears!

- Hiccups are a throwback to our amphibian ancestors that had both gills and lungs when they were tadpoles. To force water over their gills, they closed the same muscles that now produce the 'hic' in humans.

- That little pink blob in the corner of your eye is a reminder of the extra eyelid found in birds and reptiles for protecting and moistening their eyes.

🔍 SIGNS OF LIFE:

 MIRROR, MIRROR!

THE DISCOVERY OF DNA AND GENES HAS LED TO LINNAEUS'S SYSTEM (SEE PAGE 30–31) BEING CHALLENGED...

I still think mine's best!

PHYLOGENETICS

BIGGIUS HEADIUS

WHILE KEEPING GENUS AND SPECIES NAMES, SCIENTISTS ARE NOW REORDERING LIFE INTO GROUPS CALLED 'CLADES' ('CLAY-DZ') THAT INDICATE HOW AND WHEN THEY EVOLVED.

NEW WORLD MONKEYS
OLD WORLD MONKEYS
GIBBONS
ORANGUTANS
GORILLAS
CHIMPS
HUMANS

THIS SHOWS A CLADE OF APES AND PRIMATES, INCLUDING HUMANS.

OUR UNDERSTANDING OF DNA ALSO MEANS IT MIGHT PROVE POSSIBLE TO BRING BACK EXTINCT ANIMALS...

That could be a mammoth task!

Indeed!

BUT IS IT WORTH DOING WHEN SO MANY SPECIES ALIVE TODAY ARE ENDANGERED – AND WHEN SO MANY SPECIES HAVE ALREADY BECOME EXTINCT?

EXTINCTION IS A NATURAL PROCESS, AND LIFE HAS BEEN ALMOST ENTIRELY WIPED OUT SEVERAL TIMES IN THE PAST...

443 MILLION YEARS AGO, 85% OF MARINE ANIMALS LOST

G-g-g-goodbye! (SHIVER!)

375 MILLION YEARS AGO, 70% OF ALL SPECIES LOST

Goodbye! (GASP!)

252 MILLION YEARS AGO, 90% OF ALL SPECIES LOST

Goodbye! (GASP!)

66 MILLION YEARS AGO, 75% OF ALL SPECIES LOST

See you in the films...

Hope so... Help!

99.9% OF ALL LIFE EVER ON EARTH IS NOW EXTINCT.

BUT THE RATES OF EXTINCTION WE'RE SEEING TODAY HAVE BEEN HUGELY SPEEDED UP BY HUMAN ACTIVITY, AS WE'VE LEARNED FROM SEVERAL OF OUR FAVOURITE TV CONSERVATIONISTS.

JACQUES COUSTEAU, MARINE BIOLOGIST, FRANCE, 1910–1997; STEVE IRWIN, CONSERVATIONIST, AUSTRALIA, 1962–2006; DIAN FOSSEY, PRIMATOLOGIST, USA (DIED RWANDA), 1932–1985; SIR DAVID ATTENBOROUGH, NATURALIST, BORN UK, 1926.

HUMANS ARE AN INCREDIBLY CLEVER SPECIES...

Well, we invented TV for a start...

BUT OUR VERY SUCCESS NOW THREATENS THE SURVIVAL OF MANY ORGANISMS ON THE PLANET – INCLUDING US!

IN THE PAST 100 YEARS, THE NUMBER OF PEOPLE ON THE PLANET HAS RISEN 400% TO ALMOST 8 BILLION...

And you say we breed quickly!

TO FEED, FUEL AND FIND HOMES FOR ALL THESE PEOPLE, WE CONSTANTLY DESTROY NATURAL HABITATS...

Quick! Get out of here!

WE ALSO POLLUTE AND POISON THE PLANET, AND PUMP OUT CARBON THAT CAN CHANGE ITS CLIMATE.

HOWEVER, WE CAN STILL SAVE WHAT WE HAVE. AND EVERYONE CAN PLAY THEIR PART, REGARDLESS OF THEIR AGE...

It is still not too late to act!

GRETA THUNBERG, BORN SWEDEN, 2003.

REMEMBER, THERE ARE SAID TO BE MORE THAN 8 MILLION DIFFERENT SPECIES ON EARTH – MOST OF THEM STILL UNDISCOVERED. BUT ONLY ONE SPECIES HAS THE POWER TO PRESERVE THEM ALL...

WHICH ONE? LOOK IN A MIRROR!

Extinction: Dodos, Bananas and Us

Having a wide range of species living on the planet is hugely important. However, scientists reckon that up to one million species are now at risk of extinction due to human activity.

The dodo was a large flightless bird that died out on the island of Mauritius about 350 years ago. Unafraid of humans, it was probably eaten to extinction by sailors who found it an easy meal option. It lives on only in the phrase, 'As dead as a dodo'.

Sixty or so years ago, our favourite fruit almost suffered a similar fate. 'Gros Michel', then the most popular variety of banana, was struck by a fungus that caused it to wilt and die. The fungus resisted all controls and it seemed we would soon say bye-bye to bananas. Luckily, there also existed another banana variety – 'Cavendish' – that had different genes and was immune to the fungus. This is the type of banana we cultivate today.

The more, the merrier

Scientists use the term 'biodiversity' to describe the mind-melting mix of species, environments and genes encountered on Earth. Keeping the mix as rich as possible is vital. Across all seven kingdoms of living things, organisms interact to keep our little blue planet in balance.

All of these species could provide us with new foods, medicines, materials and more, as well as being fascinating and beautiful and with their own right to a place on the planet.

Help not harm

That's why we need to change. Reduce. Reuse. Recycle. Respect the environment. Plant a tree. Put in a pond. Let your lawn go wild. It isn't impossible to save what we've got, but everyone has to help. Show life some love. Frankly, it would be bananas not to!

Life Beyond Earth: Out of this World

Does life exist beyond the Earth? Yes, for sure. Look up into the sky at night and you may see the International Space Station orbiting overhead, a metal can crammed with half a dozen humans hurtling by at 27,600 kilometres per hour.

Other organisms have been up there too, including spiders, cats, monkeys, dogs, frogs, mice, rats, flies, jellyfish, guinea pigs, cockroaches, yeasts, bacteria, algae, fungi, lichens, cress, tortoises and tardigrades (seemingly indestructible micro-animals that have survived every mass extinction on Earth over the past 500 million years, and also survived the vacuum of space).

Given the endless size of the universe and the number of stars that might have hospitable planets whizzing around them, maths alone would suggest that there must be other living things out there.

We haven't found them yet. Maybe we're just looking in all the wrong places. That's life!

Glossary

amino acids: The small chemical building blocks that join together to make proteins.

antibiotic: A drug used to treat infections and diseases caused by micro-organisms, including bacteria and fungi. The first antibiotics, such as penicillin, were obtained from actual micro-organisms.

asteroid: Rocky objects that orbit the sun, as Earth does, but are much smaller than planets. Many have hit Earth in the past, and more may do so in the future.

atmosphere: The layer of gases and other vapours surrounding Earth, held in place by gravity. Today it is rich in nitrogen and oxygen, but it once contained a very different mixture of chemicals.

biodiversity: Short for 'biological diversity', this is the variety of living things, and the habitats and ecosystems they occupy. High biodiversity is important for maintaining the balance of life on our planet.

biogas: A fuel in the form of flammable gases produced by the breakdown of organic matter, including in some cases human poo! Methane is the commonest biogas.

biology: The science and study of life and all living things. Scientists who study prehistoric organisms are called palaeontologists.

botany: The science and study of plants, including their structure and naming.

carbon: A chemical element found in almost all known life on Earth and capable of forming a huge number of other compounds. Combined with oxygen, it can form carbon dioxide (CO_2), an important greenhouse gas.

chemistry: The science and study of substances ('chemicals'). It includes investigating their structures and properties, and the changes they undergo when they react with other substances.

chromosomes: DNA-containing structures, usually found in the cell nucleus, that contain the information for a cell to grow, function and reproduce. Human body cells contain 23 pairs of chromosomes, making a total of 46.

crust: The Earth's hard, rocky outer layer. It forms the continents, and continues under the oceans, although with a different composition and thickness.

DNA: Short for 'deoxyribonucleic acid', this is a molecule found in the cells of all organisms. It contains the genetic instructions for their development and function, and for making new organisms when they reproduce.

ecology: The study of how organisms interact with other living things and with their environment.

environment: The external surroundings where an organism lives. This includes other living things, as well as non-living factors such as rocks, temperature and climate. An environment can be huge – like a desert – or tiny, like the inside of a cell.

evolution: The changes in a species over several generations, caused by natural selection, which give rise to a new species with different characteristics, such as a bigger beak or different diet.

extinction: The complete dying out or end of a species. Most organisms that have ever existed are now extinct, including dinosaurs.

extremophile: An organism that thrives in an extreme environment, such as one that is very hot, highly pressurised or lacking in oxygen.

flagellum: A whip-like structure that a cell such as a bacterium uses to move around. Two or more are flagella.

fossil record: The history of life on Earth as documented by fossils. Some former living things are known only from one or two fossils. Most have left no record at all.

gene: A set sequence of special chemicals on the DNA molecule that acts as a code for a trait, grown-up height or skin colour. Genes can be passed on to offspring when organisms reproduce.

gestation: In mammals, the time between a new organism being conceived and it being born. In humans, this is about nine months.

habitat: The place where an organism lives. Different organisms and their habitats make up an ecosystem. Small, very specific dwelling places are called micro-habitats.

hydrostatic skeleton: A rigid bodily support produced by keeping water-filled structures under pressure.

hydrothermal vent: A crack in the Earth's crust on the ocean floor through which superheated water and dissolved chemicals escape.

marine: Marine organisms live alongside or in the sea or ocean.

marsupial: A type of mammal that carries and nurses its young in a pouch.

meteorite: A solid piece of space debris, such as a bit of rock from an asteroid, which hits the Earth's surface.

microbe: A living thing so small that one needs a microscope to view it, such as most bacteria and fungi.

natural selection: The process by which species change over time in response to how well they exploit their environment and compete with other organisms. The best-adapted organisms survive to reproduce ('survival of the fittest').

nucleus: In biology, this is the membrane-bound organelle inside eukaryotic cells that contains the chromosomes.

organic matter: Generally considered to be decomposing or decaying material that was once – or formed part of – a living organism, such as dead leaves on the forest floor.

organism: Any living thing.

parasite: An organism that lives in or feeds on another organism. The human head louse is one example.

prehistoric: The period before humans started writing and keeping records.

proteins: Large molecules made of amino acids. They are essential to all living things, and help to build and run their bodies. For example, fingernails are made from a protein called keratin.

pseudopod: An arm-like protrusion of the outer membrane of a protozoan such as *Amoeba*, which allows it to move and engulf food.

resistance: In biology, the ability of an organism to fight off attempts to harm or kill it. Microbes that cause disease can over time develop resistance to antibiotic drugs.

spore: A small reproductive unit that allows organisms such as bacteria, algae, fungi and some plants to spread themselves more widely.

trait: A specific characteristic of an organism coded by its genes. Traits include beak size and eye and hair colour.

zoology: The science and study of the animal kingdom.

zzzzzzzz: The koala, asleep again! (See page 56.)

Index

This book is dedicated to all those heroic
humans on page 59, and to the coelacanth –
a fin-tastic fishy survivor!

LAURENCE KING

Published by
Laurence King Publishing Ltd
361–373 City Road
London EC1V 1LR
United Kingdom
Tel: +44 20 7841 6900
E-mail: enquiries@laurenceking.com
www.laurenceking.com

© Text 2021 Mike Barfield

© Illustrations 2021 Lauren Humphrey

A catalogue record for this book is available
from the British Library

ISBN: 978-1-78627-906-4

Commissioning Editor: Leah Willey
Editor: Charlotte Selby
Design: Renata Latipova
Production: Davina Cheung

Printed in China

Laurence King Publishing is committed to
ethical and sustainable production. We are
proud participants in The Book Chain Project®
bookchainproject.com

BOOK
CHAIN
PROJECT